D0637662

A RHYME IS A TERRIBLE THING TO WASTE

306.484
J53

Nyack College Library

A RHYME
IS A TERRIBLE
THING TO WASTE

Hip Hop and the Creation
of a Political Philosophy

Carlton A. Usher

Africa World Press, Inc.

P.O. Box 1892      P.O. Box 48
Trenton, NJ 08607   Asmara, ERITREA

Africa World Press, Inc.

P.O. Box 1892
Trenton, NJ 08607

P.O. Box 48
Asmara, ERITREA

Copyright © 2006 Carlton A. Usher
First Printing 2006

All rights reserved. No part of this publication may be reproduced, stored in a retrieval system or transmitted in any form or by any means electronic, mechanical, photocopying, recording or otherwise without the prior written permission of the publisher.

Book design: Sam Saverance
Cover design: Phalon Clowers

#57893363

Library of Congress Cataloging-in-Publication Data

Usher, Carlton A.
 A rhyme is a terrible thing to waste : hip hop and the creation of a political philosophy / Carlton A. Usher.
    p. cm.
Includes bibliographical references (p.   ) and index.
ISBN 1-59221-317-0 (hardcover) -- ISBN 1-59221-318-9 (pbk.)
 1. Hip-hop--Political aspects. 2. Hip-hop--Religious aspects. 3. Rap
(Music) I. Title.

ML3531.U85 2005
306.4'84249--dc22

*Your belief system ain't louder
than my car system*

— Penny for a thought, Saul Williams

TABLE OF CONTENTS

List of Tables and Illustrations   ix

Acknowledgments   xi

Chapter I: Introduction   **1**
Background   1
The Problem   2
Marginality as Centrality   4
Definition of Terms   12

Chapter II: Schools of Thought   **15**
Historical Continuity and Hip- Hop Culture   18
Black Nationalism and HC   21
Post Industrial Politics and Hip- Hop Culture   25
Hip Hop as Art   31

Chapter III: Black Theology and Hip Hop Culture   **33**
Black Theology, Political Philosophy, and the Evolution of HC   34
The Nation of Islam   37
The Nation of Gods and Earths and Father Allah   38
Post-Industrialism, the NOI, NGE, and the Emergence of HC   40
Political Theory, NOI, NGE, and HC   43
Statement of Ideals, the NOI, NGE, and HC   46
Agencies, the NOI, NGE, and HC   50
Ideology, NOI, NGE, and HC   54
Ethic, NOI, NGE, and HC   59

Chapter IV: God Is Hip Hop   65
Christian Hip Hop: An Oxymoron   65
Living Water or Iced Out   69

Chapter V: HC and the Political Economy of Black Radio   73
History of Black Radio   73
Black Radio and the Crisis of Function   74
Black Radio and The Telecommunications Act of 1996   76
Atlanta Black Radio Case Studies   77
WRFG: "The Voice of the Atlanta Community"   77
WRAS- 88.5 (Georgia State University Radio)   80
Control Formats, Industry Trade Publications and HC   82
WHTA (Hot 97.5) "Doing Good in the Hood"   85
WVEE- 103 -"The people station"   88
Conclusion   90

Chapter VI: Underground Hip Hop Culture   93
Historical Overview of Underground HC   94
UHC and "Didactic Nihilism": A Response to Self Destruction   96
UHC and Public Space: A Response to Spacial Control   98
UHC and Capitalism: A Response to Perceived Exploitation   105

Chapter VII: School Daze: Perceptions and Political Values in   113
Hip Hop
Ideology and Perceptions of American Politics   114
Trust and the Political Process   119
HC and Political Potential   120
Summary   123

Chapter VIII: Government Mule: The Political System and Hip   125
Hop Culture

HC and the Shaping of Public Policy   126
HC's Adversaries and the Political System   128
Conclusions and Recommendations   131

Notes   133

Works Cited   151

Index   157

LIST OF TABLES
AND ILLUSTRATIONS

Tables

1. Compilation Albums   54
2. Top Ten Radio Groups   76
3. NLR Sales Estimates   84
4. Income Generated from Rap Sales   107
5. Sample Size and Institution   114
6. Issues of Concern   115

Illustrations

1. African American Islam   35
2. Nation of Islam Chart   38
3. Flag of the NGE   44
4. Nation of Islam   44
5. Traditional Model   108
6. Discussion of political problems   115
7. Government responsibility for eliminating poverty   116
8. Public welfare programs   116
9. Political system and the wealthy   117
10. Generations of slavery and discrimination   118
11. Blacks can improve their conditions by voting   118
12. Government officials and Hip Hop artists   119
13. Black elected officials and power   120
14. Hip Hop, partying, and politics   120
15. Political messages in Hip Hop   121
16. Hip Hop Culture is about getting paid   122
17. Artist and their communities   122
18. Hip Hop and African- Americans   123

ACKNOWLEDGEMENTS

Thanks to all my family for their loving support especially my sister Cynthia for all her unconditional encouragement. Thanks to my mother Alma for showing me what determination really is. Thank you to my son Mzuri for sharing his wisdom and insights. Thanks to Rebecca King, Rechelle and David Fears for their support and patience. Many thanks to Dedra Thornton and the Thornton Family for giving me all their love and support.

Special thanks to my friends Dr. Melanie Richburg, Dr. Alison Ligon, the Alvarado family, Dr. Perry Thornton, Dr. Laurie Rodgers, Dr. Kurt Young, Dr. Timothy Moore, Dr. Howard Grant, Jartu Toles, Eric Hall, Kenny Groves, Dr. Ketema Paul, Dr. Al Harmon, Hafeez Wootson, Phalon Clowers, David Washington, Maurice Francis, Al Nottage, James Jordan, and the men in Omega Psi Phi Fraternity.

Without the help of some mentors my efforts would be minimal. Thanks to Dr. Mack H. Jones, Dr. William Boone, Dr. Russell Irvine, Dr. James Young, Dr. Hashim Gibrill, Dr. Keith Baird, Dr. Michael Gomez, Dr. Robin Kelley, and Dr. Marvin Hare.

Special thanks to all the wonderful colleagues at Morehouse College, Kennesaw State University, Clark Atlanta University, Spelman College, Lincoln University, Howard University, and Virginia State University. Thanks to all my wonderful friends at Africa World Press for their patience and meticulous work on my behalf.

I wrote this in honor of all of those young men and women trying to develop new paradigms and political philosophies.

Chapter I
INTRODUCTION

Background

Patricia Williams once remarked: "For blacks describing needs has been a dismal failure as a political activity. It has succeeded only as a literary achievement."[1] This "success" is reflected in a myriad of African-American cultural productions, hereafter referred to as AACP. From art, cinema, music and a list of dynamic cultural productions the assumption is made that participation in American culture via creative expression is synonymous with progress. That is to say, confusion surrounds the notion that the ability to produce has the same value as the culture product itself. A study of political history provides us with numerous examples of such miscalculations and the attempts to ratify them.

The "Art v. Propaganda" crisis of the Harlem Renaissance provided one such example. Some producers of culture believed that the art forms and artists must be courageous and clearly make political statements. Otherwise their product was useless.

The Negro artist worked against an undertow of sharp criticism and misunderstanding from his own group and unintentional bribes from whites. "Oh, be respectable, write about nice people, show how good we are," say the Negroes. "Be stereotyped, don't go too far, don't shatter our illusions about you, and don't amuse us too seriously. "We will pay you."[2]

Others reasoned that truth should play a secondary role to beauty. This argument rests on the assumption that the creation of a "New Negro" is, in essence, political.[3] This position is limited because "beauty" can never address poverty, unemployment, racial violence and other harsh realities of black life during the turn of the century. Marcus Mosiah

Garvey understood the dilemma. His race first ideology stressed the necessity for Africans to recognize their beauty, but also recognized that art and artists should reflect a political philosophy consistent with the aims and goals of the Universal Negro Improvement Association (UNIA). Thus he and others in the organization did not hesitate to denounce artists who did not project their race and class philosophy. In fact, "a literary censor was recommended who would safeguard black people from material unfavorable to the race."[4]

The sixties movement reflected much of the same. The productions of Larry Neal, Haki Madhubuti, Gwendolyn Brooks, Nikki Giovanni, Amiri Baraka, Sonia Sanchez and a multitude of others challenged the purpose and utility of cultural creations and creativity. As Baraka stated,

> The Art is the National Spirit. That manifestation of it. Black Art must be the Nationalist's vision given more form and feeling, as a raiser [sic] to cut away what is not central to National Liberation. To show that which is.[5]

The assessment of African-American empowerment has been in part historically measured in terms of cultural production that reflects protest against or support for integration into American society. These two competing ideologies and a multitude of others are not exclusive to representation in the arts, but the arts provide platforms where these ideas are broadcast, scrutinized and/or rationalized and, more importantly, made accessible to the general population.

The Problem

The cultural production of African-Americans has dominated the American landscape. As a result, critical assessment of black life and culture that point to successes in the arts erroneously assumes that participation in cultural production is synonymous with political participation. This is not to say that the attempts to codify, verify, and modify the black political landscape through political activity (scholarship and participation) are less valuable. However, the increased reliance on AACP as the explanatory device to describe the status of black life in America serves not only as a reminder of the failure of assertive politics, as is suggested, but seems to be moving to replace it. Control needs are more frequently magnified via the arts. As a result, political assessments of African-American culture must include scrutiny of their cultural production to analyze if in fact the cultural products possess "political utility."[6] It becomes a much more urgent task since historically some semblance of political sentiments is contained in the cultural production. When it becomes a universal commodity for capitalist enterprise, the utility of cultural production is marginalized and its function becomes subversive to the continued development of cohesive political strategies connected to race, class, and gender. As such, the semblance of political utility found in contemporary AACP must be further investigated. Such an investigation will answer whether in fact the AACP describe political reality and prescribe strategies for transformation. These products may in fact be too trivial and devoid of any political relevance for a case regarding political utility to be made.

Globally, American cultural identity is disproportionately dependent on and depicted by one of its more marginalized ethnic groups, the African-American. Some corporations have capitalized on AACP by presenting diverse segments of African life and culture in America as monolithic. This translates to more opportunities for a minute segment of African America, the artists as producer. Their participation is multi-functional; it has dual purpose. It serves as an opportunity for employment of some whose contribution to society would otherwise be minimal and in some cases adversarial. It also serves as evidence to those who attempt to justify the position that all is well in the general society and that liberal democratic ideals are realized. Of greater concern for this research is the utility of these apparent artistic and creative successes specifically created by African-Americans in the attempt to clarify and remediate political needs of the people responsible for such cultural creations. For example we were told a few years ago that "more books by and about African-Americans will be published this year than appeared during the whole of the Harlem Renaissance."[7] While this must and should be viewed as an achievement, the majority of these culture products will yield more capital for the investor than the producer. In addition, what production is funded is too often a reflection of the politics of the investor.[8]

The dilemma regarding the purpose and function of African-American cultural production remains a crucial issue. A careful critique of Hip Hop Culture, hereafter referred to as (HC), will determine whether the dilemma of the Harlem Renaissance and the Sixties remains a major area of crisis and contention. Presently, HC presented in its one-dimensional form serves to undermine the evolution of useful political descriptions in much the same way that the above-mentioned movements of the past had. What is presented is a one-dimensional image of African youth, consumerism as empowerment that camouflages class relationships and wealth inequality. bell hooks' argument that commodification is not synonymous with self determination is accepted and useful as a critique of the failure to adequately address the issue raised here. She states:

> I would add that the contemporary commodification of blackness has become a dynamic part of that system of cultural repression. Opportunistic longings for fame, wealth, and power now lead many black critical thinkers, marketing of black culture in ways that are complicit with the existing oppressive structure. That complicity begins with the equating of black capitalism with black self-determination.[9]

Marginality as Centrality

The aphorism that states, if you are not part of the solution, you are part of the problem, is a discerning description of the dynamism regarding the dilemma in HC. Clichés such as "the children are the future" become empty rhetoric if we continue to ignore how culture affects them as well as how they affect culture. I contend that it would be more effective to identify what factors within HC leads to de-politicizing, that is, the continued downward spiral of youth culture's confidence in political awareness and participation as a viable method of problem solving. In addition, if HC does provide alternative political views, they too, must be identified. This must occur as a precursor to an attempt to describe the control needs of a people. HC is the most integrative cultural product post 1960s. Claims that it is rebellious and oppositional to the generally accepted ideals of American democracy remain an exaggeration. Its potential to be used as a progressive tool for empowering African-American youth is acknowledged but has not been actualized because it is rebellious, confrontational and often its prescriptive elements are rarely mass produced or have mass appeal. The following statement though not a specific reference to HC supports the point here. One well- known African-American author states:

> There have been titanic changes, and they have been accompanied by unexpected ironies. The most striking change has been the growing centrality of the black experience to the maturing national culture of the United States; the most striking irony has been the degree to which blacks, despite that centrality, have remained economically marginal.[10]

This marginalization may be a direct result of the centrality, yet not a "striking irony" of it. The centrality of the black experience in the United States is simply a reflection of market and consumer culture. It does not reflect the making of common decision for a group of people through the exercise of power, which is the basis of political activity. Nor does it cause others to yield to the wishes of African-America, which is the basis of power itself. The centrality of the black experience, as well as its marginalization, are both symptoms of the historical dilemma of the matrix of race and class. The one-dimensional depictions of AACP especially in HC exacerbate both symptoms by presenting marginalization as centrality. Each time we celebrate "the first black" to achieve some goal we are reminded of this confusion. To determine whether aspects of HC presented as centrality is in fact marginalization, I would ask: If the African art form of Hip Hop, is a viable political instrument.

By viable political instrument I mean a set of assumptions and ideas that enhance the ability of HC adherents to describe the ongoing social order and their place in it, to chose between alternative futures and to develop strategies and tactics for pursuing the desired future. To determine whether HC is a viable political instrument, there must be a number of preliminary questions.

First, is religion a key component regarding HC's politics? The historical importance and value of religion as a political instrument is a common thread in the political experience of African-Americans. Since the voluntary and involuntary arrival of Africans in America, religion has been an instrument of politics. Whether it was used as a tool to control or liberate the enslaved, provide moral suasion for abolitionist, or the driving force behind the Civil Rights movement, religion's utility is unquestionable. It historically, many strategies and philosophies attempting to address pertinent issues affecting America's Africans have relied on religion as a driving force. If HC is a political instrument that emanates from the African experience in America, this sub culture should be scrutinized to see if it reflects historical continuity of religion as a political instrument. At issue here is whether HC as a rebel culture still operates within the paradigm of the historical connection between religions as politics to address African concerns. A possible link between the development of its religious ideology as the driving force behind its politics cannot be ignored. I am prepared to argue that HC's resistance to traditional Christian religious ideology means that it was built on a religious foundation, albeit directly opposes, contradicts, and, at times ridicules Christianity.

Second, is black radio a viable political instrument? Black radio, similar to the black press, has historically served as the voice of people rendered voiceless by Jim Crow, racism and discrimination. Black radio has provided African-America with perspectives and information that challenges the general societal position of its most marginalized citizens, Africans in America. The utility of radio promoted as "black" is severely threatened. With relatively few exceptions, those still in existence have been described as generally working against the interest of Africans in America. One of black radio's most vocal critics, Chuck D, puts it best. He states that "of all these radio stations that play Black Music people don't realize that a very small percentage of those radio stations are black owned."[11] Chuck D adds that the primary decision makers are radio consultants who are detached from the black communities' needs.

> In the 1980s the large corporations started taking over the radio stations and as a result, the Black seems to come out of everything. That's when it became "more music. Less talk." Program directors must have started getting instructions from higher up to tell the disc jockeys to shut up. If you shut up the deejay, then you're left with an unclear picture of what the music is really about. All of a sudden the music becomes the only communicator, and the music isn't always the best communicator.[12]

This position is highlighted by Chuck D's assertion that those programming consultants have no link or cultural connection to the large audience that black radio enjoys. Ultimately decisions are solely based on the marketplace and the broadcasting of political concerns are virtually nonexistent. Therefore, to investigate black radio stations that present rap music as part of their programming is necessary to understand if black radio is an adversary of politicized HC or works against it.

Third, is HC's underground a politically viable institution? As a result of the commodification of HC, some have called for establishing an autonomous culture space, commonly referred to as the "underground." It is comprised of artists on independent labels and organizations that attempt to function as the authentic if not alternative voice of HC. These agencies together form an elaborate system of checks and balances regarding what is acceptable as an authentic reflection of HC. They function as a method of communication devoid of commercial interests. In fact the underground has in many cases been most critical of mainstream interactions between HC and the general public. Many successful artists boast that their careers started in the underground but ironically are usually verbally trashed by it once acceptance by the general audience has occurred. Within the underground, culture products, which may provide challenges to western world views, are determined "unmarketable" and discarded by traditional modes of production and distribution (multi-national corporations). Disdain for the marketplace and commercial HC has produced an underground in most major cities. Their cultural creations are usually[13] political by design and in many cases chastise mainstream artists for falsely depicting what they perceive to be black reality. As a result, the underground provides not only a critique of mainstream HC but in many cases is responsible for creating an alternative culture product to counter the mainstream. Therefore, to present a study of the underground community to decide whether a political philosophy exists is also necessary.

Fourth, do participants in HC recognize its potential political viability? As a culture product HC's impact is far reaching. It touches nearly every aspect of American life. From mainstream to the margins, this art form has impacted the lives of Americans, and it has provided a voice for some and represents dissonance for others. That said, a cursory investigation of HC reveals a vacuum between politicized aspects of HC and its audience. A more detailed examination will tell us whether this observation is valid and can be supported with corresponding evidence.

Fifth, is HC disengaged from the political process? Policy makers within the political landscape who attempt to sway loyalty, shape policy and advance their agenda use multi- modal strategies. Among these policy makers are liberals and conservatives, both of whom reference black cultural expression to support their agenda. These examples are usually unfavorable representations of urban culture, the so-called ghetto, where young African-Americans are the central focus group. Consistent with Africans in America in general, aspects of HC have been and continue to be used as wedge issues in the political process. Welfare fraud, crime, voluntary unemployment and a list of other societal ills are associated with HC in the same manner they are connected to Africans in America. This is more apparent at the state and national levels. What is virtually ignored is HC's attempt usually at the local and regional level to affect change. Major labels and artists do in fact participate in the political process. The effectiveness of such participation is in some cases marginal and in others effective. Therefore, to investigate the political evolution, development and execution of programs and projects generated by HC that attempt to affect change is useful. Dismissing HC's attempt to affect political outcomes possibly can perpetuate the legitimacy of the one-dimensional depictions[14] of African America, aid in the development of policies that do little to remedy the failure of liberal democracy and undermine the effort of those within HC who are attempting to make a change. To respond adequately to this question it is necessary to catalogue hearings, court cases, public policy, bills and laws that are directly associated with HC to determine the position of members in the political system regarding HC and whether they are consistent with the general view of African culture in America. More important, it will tell us where some of the obstacles exist within the political process that may impede HC's attempt to affect change and qualify as a viable political instrument.

The central question posed by this research is whether HC is a viable political instrument that can be used to influence political behavior of its adherents in some desired direction. For HC to be a viable political instrument, it must contain a political philosophy that allows its followers to ascribe meaning to particular situations and determine appropriate courses of action. To determine whether HC embodies a political philosophy, I should begin by defining the term. Drawing on the works of C. Wright Mills and Jones, one can conceptualize a political philosophy as a set of assumptions that provides a basis for deciding the nature of existing political reality, how it came into being and a desirable political future. According to Mills, political philosophies include theories that suggest how society came into being, how it is made up, what are its major areas of consensus and cleavage, and how societal conflicts are resolved and in whose interests: ideals that designate the societal goals to be pursued; historical agencies through which ideals are to be pursued; and ideologies used to attract, mobilize, and exhort supporters. More useful for this research is Jones' summary of categories provided by Mills. Jones presents these elements as "constituent elements" of a political philosophy, which also include ethics. Jones presents these elements as follows: theories, statement of ideals; statements of historical agencies; ideology and ethic. He states,

> Taken together, as an integrated philosophy, these
> elements provide a basis for interpreting political
> reality, prescribing the desired future, determining
> what practices and institutions would be the appro-
> priate structures for pursuing that future, and for
> evaluating the people and the institutions involved in
> the enterprise.[15]

These elements along with Jones' integrative description
serve as the basis for defining the phrase "viable political instrument." This methodological structure relies on defining political
viability. The overall emphasis is restricted to those aspects of
HC as defined.

Once the term political philosophy is defined and opera-
tional, a next step is to determine if a political philosophy is
embedded in HC. In order to make that determination, I will
conduct a historical analysis of the genesis of HC to determine if
there are any particular cultural or political forces that condition
its beginning and, if so, if they are grounded in any particular
philosophy. A review of the literature and preliminary research
reveals that two religious organizations, the Nation of Islam and
the Nations of God and Earth, serve as cultural and spiritual
incubators for a number of the founding member-artists of HC.
Accordingly, I conduct case studies of these two organizations
and their impact on the evolution of HC to determine whether
they subscribe to an identifiable political philosophy.

My case study confirms that both organizations have distinct
but similar political philosophies and that a number of prominent
HC artists are affiliated with these organizations and subscribe
to their philosophies. A content analysis of the lyrics of selected
artists to determine whether the lyrics reflect ideas embedded in
these philosophies.

We should also want to know whether young people who
embrace HC see it as a political instrument and recognize its
political potential. Toward that end, I conduct a random survey
of entering freshmen at the Atlanta University Center institutions
to determine their perceptions of HC as a political instrument.
While freshmen entering the Atlanta University Center institutions may not be representative of the entire community, the

survey may not allow me to establish external validity. However, given the fact that the entering freshmen are typically between eighteen and twenty years old and given the fact that the students hail from throughout the United States with disproportionate representation from the large urban centers where HC is especially strong, the results of the Atlanta University Center students can provide s a defensible basis for discussing the attitudes of HC adherents.

The viability of HC as a political instrument, of course, is determined to a great extent by the conduit through which it reaches the preponderance of its adherents: that is, radio, particularly what is called black or urban radio. To determine the extent to which radio and related activities enhance or detract from HC's potential political viability, I analyze four Atlanta radio stations that played HC music, two commercial and two non-profit radio stations. I also conduct interviews with station personnel and content analyses of station play lists to determine the extent to which stations play political oriented music and otherwise motivate their listeners to become involved politically.

A literature review and preliminary research also reveal the existence of an underground HC, both nationally and internationally, that nurtures and provides space for autonomous voices that are independent of mainstream commercial HC. This underground culture is by it own acknowledgment consciously political and as such should enhance the potential political viability of HC. To determine if this is true, I examine both the Atlanta and national underground communities to assess their contributions to the political viability of HC. Specifically, I examine the lyrical content of selected artists to determine what political philosophy they reflect. I also investigate their efforts to secure public space for their performances and related activities and the response of authorities to their efforts. Finally, I analyze their efforts to disengage themselves from the dominant record and entertainment industry by establishing alternative ownership and control of their cultural products.

Definition of Terms

There are five concepts used in this study that require additional explanation. They are Hip Hop culture, African-American cultural production, viable political instrument, the underground, and the political system. "Hip Hop culture" refers to the youth driven African-American sub-culture with street derived elements that evolved around the production of new music forms in the latter decades of the twentieth century. These elements include "MCing" or "Emceeing," that is, combining street vernacular and distinct drum rhythms to create a music form commonly identified as Hip Hop. Other elements include "Breakin'" or "Breakdancing," and "DJing," which is the process of manipulating music tempo through methods identified as mixing, scratching and cutting. The culture is, of course, more than one musical form, but a collection of styles, beliefs and behaviors evinced by those associated with the genesis, evolution and preservation of the phenomenon. Like other cultural moments such as bohemian or generation X, Hip Hop culture cannot be defined with scientific precision but its existence as a significant social force is beyond challenge.

"African-American cultural" production refers to the tangible and intangible products in literature, visual arts, music, dance and the oral tradition produced by people of African descent who hold special relevance for African-American culture. In this study I am primarily concerned with products related to music, dance and oral traditions.

Commodification is the process through which a culture product's autonomy is reduced to a casualty of capitalism such that its significance is determined fundamentally if not solely by its exchange value. The commodification process highlights the interaction between voluntary and involuntary involvement of cultural producers, cultural products and the hegemonic dominance of capitalism. I accept Marx's notion that commodification has only negative and destructive consequence. Human labor as well as the product of that labor is a commodity. Marx interprets labor as well as its products as essential to capitalist development. Such interactions diminish the human to the status of a commodity.[16] In contemporary society every product has the potential to be co-modified. The area where conflict is articulated rests in the judgment regarding whether the commodity is "uncontested" or "contested." The former describes the acceptance, the latter describes the challenge of the process of commodification.[17] For this study the classification "contested" is accepted as the primary concern. Consequently, commodification is not solely the theoretical construct of value or the practice of placing value. Commodification encompasses both. The definitive demarcation exists at the point of contestation at which the decision to resist does or does not exist. Many examples regarding contestation, though not limited to issues of ethics, are more apparent in this area. For instance, commodification is contested regarding the sale of children, sex, the sale of human body parts to the highest bidder and, more recently, the reproduction of vital organs for body transplant surgery.

"Underground" refers to a subculture of HC where voices are autonomous, capitalism has not interfered with the cultural products, and descriptions and prescriptions with regard to American life are uninfluenced by the general society. This term's origin is in direct accord with the Hip Hop community's recognition that its cultural products were co-opted in the late nineteen eighties by corporatism and profit driven motives. The underground represents a counteraction against such incorporations. This subculture sees its cultural products as authentic for they respond less to the marketplace and are more concerned with tradition, self-determination and in many cases, self-chastisement.

The term "political system," is defined by Easton as a "set of interactions abstracted from the totality of social behavior, through which values are authoritatively allocated for a society."[18] It is the mechanism through which present political interactions and HC will be analyzed. I consider all aspects of the political system as they correspond to the affairs of America's Africans but my primary focus is on the environment, its inputs and outputs. Easton describes "inputs" as demanding, and "outputs" as emanating from the political system in the form of decision and policy actions. Environment is the "rest" of society.[19] For this study, environment is important in that AACP emanates from it and is therefore the station where inputs may be defined. These include political positions of elected officials, policy intention(s) and outcome(s). The political process and the state also help shape this definition.

"Viable political instrument" is a set of ideas and assumptions that can be used by adherents to describe the existing social order and their place in it, to identify and discriminate among competing alterative views of the desired future, and to develop strategies and tactics for pursuing the desired future.

Chapter II
SCHOOLS OF THOUGHT

Scholarship regarding the unique thirty-year old African cultural product of Hip Hop offers a prescriptive and descriptive assessment of youth culture. The centrality of HC in contemporary American culture has created a virtual scramble by writers of diverse disciplines or orientations to write about HC. Most of these works are devoid of epistemological structures that would allow us to distinguish between the positive and negative dimensions of HC. Much of the writing is deficient because it lacks a systematic, theoretical orientation. There is a need for such an orientation because it can clearly indicate, the normative assumptions that the writers have regarding HC and the broader American culture.

Mack H. Jones offers a critique of social science which, while not specific to HC, illuminates the present crisis. Jones identifies the process of social science inquiry by delineating between two distinct stages, the consciously normative and the objective or scientific dimension. According to Jones:

> The consciously normative includes (1) the process in which we confront the world of sense perceptions of what is external to us as observers, which F. S. C. Northrop has labeled the world of pure fact (Northrop:1969, 35-38); (2) the normative rules prescribed by the culture of the people in question for giving meaning to sense perceptions; or to put it differently, the socially sanctioned rules for converting the world of pure fact into described fact; (3) the

development of social science disciplines in response
to the anticipation and control needs of the people in
question: (4) the development of paradigms within
which communities of scholars work; (5) the construction of frames of reference to guide problem
formulation prescribe the level of analysis, determine
the criteria of evidence and stipulate the appropriate methods and techniques to be used; and (6) the
determination of which regularities constitute "problems." All of these are purposive and normative.[20]

Jones argues that the substantive content of a people's social
science is developed by normative assumptions when knowing
begins; not by science. As a result, "the consciously normative
phase merits equal if not greater attention and understanding
because it is the consciously normative operations that render all
social science inquiry parochial and idiosyncratic to the culture
from which it emanates."[21]

My position that HC is a subject of social science cannot be
fully understood until elements that constitute the "consciously
normative" are considered. Such a requirement is necessary
because it allows studies of HC to develop models, paradigms
and frameworks to examine its essence. Studies in social science
regarding HC have barely developed "the construction of frames
of reference to guide problem formulation, prescribe the level
of analysis, determine the criteria of evidence and stipulate the
appropriate methods and techniques to be used." A framework
becomes a vehicle to determine which aspects of HC "constitute problems," whereby a course of action can be established.
The following example serves as a theoretical device with special
utility for studying HC. This also demonstrates why the development of a framework is necessary.

In examining the *Colonial Model* as an explanatory device that
illustrates the position of black America, the following is known:

The black community is pictured as the object of
cultural imperialism dating back to slavery and continuing with the appropriation and commodification
of black cultural forms during the present epoch. The
ability of the black colony to mobilize its resources

and particularly its human resources for effective political struggle is undermined by the destruction of its cultural base.[22]

Using this normative model as a frame of reference for analyzing, HC illuminates several useful theses. First, HC is a response to cultural imperialism. Second, HC aids in cultural imperialism. Or third, HC is not affected by cultural imperialism and/or vice versa. Using this model allows a decision about whether any of these explanations offers an opportunity to determine HC's function(s). More important, HC rumored as a mode through which a rudimentary black politics exists, must be connected to models that attempt to explain what black politics *is*. Appropriately, if the problems that HC confronts are historical by nature, previously established paradigms that attempt to address these historical problems must be accepted or at least included. Ultimately the development of new approaches resulting from existing approaches such as the "colonial model" will coincide with the new varieties of culture products that attempt to add to "the process of deciding what configurations of regularities constitute historical problems." In this case, HC. New varieties of culture product that can be seen as emancipation vehicles must also be developed via academic and scholastic orientations.

Scholarship regarding HC has attempted to initiate new frameworks, but most are not directly related to political viability. There are a few exceptions. For instance Pamela D. Hall offers a compelling study of rap music and its possible effects on the memory of children between seven and twelve years of age. Her findings are worthy repeating. She writes:

> The recall findings show that younger children may not be able to describe what the music is about. However, the recognition data suggests that they do have a general understanding of the music. The results show that older children are better at describing the message of all types of music on recall and recognition. The result show that older children are better at describing the message of all types of rap songs except commercial rap. Commercial rap music may be the most popular type of rap music in that it may be

played or heard on the radio more often then other
forms of rap music. [23]

She also states, unlike gangsta, hip-hop and political rap
the message of commercial rap may not be as difficult to comprehend. The only type of rap music that showed an age difference in recognition memory was gangsta rap music. The finding
suggests that gangsta rap may be more difficult to understand
for younger people. This study has relevance for several reasons.
First, vehicles responsible for the normative development of
youth must be identifiable, because they shape a worldview.
Trying to socialize children through politicized HC, one should
know (at what age) socialization of youth occurs is relevant.
Second, knowing what agency(ies) are effective and ineffective
is also crucial. Third, understanding the aspects of HC that children are more likely to memorize allows for judgment to be made
regarding exposure and access. Fourth, if "political rap" is more
difficult to comprehend and commercial rap from play is not,
agencies such as radio that deliver these apolitical forms must
be held more accountable. Thus, the development of a political
strategy void of emotionalism to address accountability is justifi-
able. The empirical evidence would provide the platform.

Other literature that offers constructive methodologies
regarding useful approaches to comprehend HC fall under three
main categories. This is not to say that only these categories exist,
but that they represent the most frequently used frameworks
for understanding HC. These are historical continuity, black
nationalism and post industrialism. The majority of research that
attempts to examine the political dynamics of HC uses one or
more of these approaches to do so.

Historical Continuity and Hip Hop Culture

This frame of reference for analyzing HC recommends that
it should be conceptualized as a contemporary episode of historical continuity. Unstable historical interactions between America
and its Africans, the political climate such interactions create, and
new cultural forms as weapons of resistance form the essence of
this continuity. HC represents a new culture form responding
to a historical crisis. Jazz, Blues, Soul, Rock and Roll, and, pres-

ently HC, have all attempted to offer politicized products that reflect and respond to the political climate. All these forms have experienced the crisis of incorporation. Several authors frame the evolution of HC within this context.

Mark Anthony Neal, in *What the Music Said: Black Popular Music and Black Public Culture* interpolates the history of Black America with new forms of technology and demonstrates the manner in which these forms affect and reflect the politics of each era. Beginning with the turn of the century and continuing to the end of the millennium, Neal demonstrates how the inter-action of technology, politics and culture impact black life. Cultural products were created in part, as a response to segregation and racism. Technology allowed these forms, especially music, to be mass-produced. The political climate and the owners of the technology dictated which aspects would be mass-produced. Those cultural products and producers deemed less threatening to the social order benefited. Neal focuses on intransigent black artists who challenged the oppressive institutions in the society and who consequently saw their careers abruptly diminished. Neal's concern is that popular black culture's crisis of commodity must be viewed in its politicized historical context as an on going dialectic. This is a relevant approach since I am investigating HC, which is a thirty-year old response to a four hundred year old crisis. In addition, it presents evidence that such crises are systemic and not sporadic or contemporary. The challenges within HC are similar if not exact to those of the jazz, blues, soul, funk and rhythm and blues.[24] Black youth played, and continue to play a pivotal in shaping black culture.

S. Craig Watkins presents a historical analysis. He asserts that due to a lack of discretionary income prior to the fifties, no real substantive relationship between black youth, the popular industrial image-making landscape, and a rapidly evolving cultural marketplace developed.[25] A visible shift came in the 1950s. Watkins asserts,

> It was also during the fifties and sixties when the rela-
> tionship between black youth and the popular culture
> industry began to take shape in earnest, correspond-
> ing with rising black incomes, the wider distribution

of television, the transformation of black appeal
radio, and the creation of an elaborate "star system"
made possible by promotional vehicles like Motown,
Soul Train, and Black teen magazines.[26]

In an article titled "Hip Hop 101" in *Droppin Science*,
Robert Farris Thompson locates cross cultural connections as a
pivotal element if one is to understand the evolution of Hip Hop
in its fullness. Thompson reasons that Congo Square in New
Orleans provided the earliest signs of cultural continuities that
ultimately led to Hip Hop's formation. Similar to others who
define HC as a contemporary offspring of African culture continuity, Thompson briefly traces the evolution of the predecessors
such as soul and funk and which ultimately led to Hip Hop.[27] He
further stresses the diverse ethnicities and their musical variations
that existed prior to Hip Hop's development that were valuable
contributors. Central to Thompson's thesis is that the cultures
of North American blacks, Barbadian, Jamaicans and Cubans to
name a few, represent the nucleus in the development of a form
called Hip Hop. His position is fortified with evidence which
reveals the majority of those identified as Hip Hop's founders
were from diverse ethnic backgrounds with common African
cultural elements at their core. These common elements of the
various cultures such as (drums, rhythm and vocal patterns) are
the essence of Hip Hop. HC is more politicized through language than any other forms of communicative expression such
as graffiti, dance or dress. HC's defining essence as rebellious
is located in its ability to adopt new language in a seemingly
perpetual tempo. For its advocates, HC presents temporal space
where participation in language/culture exchanges and communication that articulates social and political concerns, occurs
with a degree of autonomy. Its creation, understanding and
acceptance are understood almost exclusively by its creators.[28]
Hip Hop predecessors such as spirituals, the blues, jazz and soul
are described in a similar manner. Thus studies which attempt
to investigate the ways in which HC is shaped by and affects
language are vital for they illustrate historical continuity.

Such scholarship offering historical continuity as an explanatory device, while valuable, does highlight a discrepancy. If HC

is a product of cultural continuity and this product contains ominous destructive elements, it is the culture at large that is problematic. HC is merely its latest manifestation. Thus, the need to frame HC within a larger context such as Black Nationalism is necessary, but advocates must be prepared to confront these ominous features in their approach.

Black Nationalism and HC

Politicized rap music is overwhelmingly attached to Black Nationalism. Many advocates of the fusion between Black Nationalism and HC use the words of its more politicized artists to make their case. For instance the lyrics of Public Enemy, KRS-1, X-Clan and a host of other artists affiliated with Nationalist organizations such as the Nation of Islam[29] are used to make the connection. According to many, Black Nationalism grew from one of three historical phases in the development of HC.

Hip Hop as traditionally defined originated in the Bronx, New York. Joseph Sadler, also known as (Grandmaster Flash), is viewed as one of its most significant pioneers. Other significant founders include Clive Campbell (DJ Kool Herc) and Afrika Bambaataa. Nelson George informs us that Hip Hop was sparked by a few pioneering men on the streets of New York City via block parties and jams in public parks. He continues,

> On their wheels of steel Kool Herc, Afrika Bambaataa, and Grandmaster Flash staked out a loud, scratchy, in-your face aesthetic that, to this day, still informs the culture. But it didn't come out of nowhere-- no spontaneous generation of this deadly virus. The b-boys-the dancers, graffiti writers, the kids just hanging out, who carried the hip hop attitude forth were reacting to disco, to funk, and the chaotic world of New York City in the '70s. These b-boys (and girls) were mostly black and Hispanic. They were hip hop's first generation. They were America's first post-soul kids.[30]

These post-soul kids introduced a style of dance, music, art, poetry, politics and dress within black communities that spread rapidly throughout America within a relatively short period of

time. The earliest manifestation of their effort was called breaking; a mixture of martial arts, dance and raw athleticism. This
constituted the first wave in the development of HC. It included
graffiti, braggadocios rap, the dozens and turntable mixing.
William Eric Perkins lists gangsta rap and political rap as its next
two phases.[31] It is within the latter phase or wave that Black
Nationalism is located. Perkins demonstrates the existence of
Black Nationalism within HC by describing the ideology of both
Public Enemy and the Nation of Islam. Perkins suggests that this
form of political rap is responsible for the emergence of Black
Nationalism within rap culture.[32] Another writer lists the second
and third stages of HC as commercial rap and political awareness
rap, respectively. The former saw the rise in new artists and the
societal perception that rap music is violent. The latter, political
awareness, led to the development of Black Nationalism.[33] An
equally useful assessment provided by Errol A. Henderson uti-
lizes Maulana Karenga's definition of Black Nationalism. Black
Nationalism is defined as,

> The political belief and practice of African-Americans
> as a distinct people with a distinct historical person-
> ality who politically should develop structures to
> define, defend, and develop the interest of Blacks as
> a people. This entails a redefinition of reality in Black
> images and interests, providing a social corrective, by
> building institutions and organizational structures
> that house Black aspirations, and it provides a collec-
> tive vocation of nation building among Black people
> as a political end. [34]

Henderson suggests that there are three justifications for the
emergence of Black Nationalism:

> First is the brand of nationalism that emerges from
> identification rooted in a perceived commonality of
> oppression. Another emerges from a recognition of
> a convergence of political purpose, objectives, and
> goals. Third is the brand of nationalism that rest on
> the justification of a commonality of culture. [35]

Henderson believes that all three brands of nationalism are found within rap music and that the latter have been more visible as rap became more politically sophisticated. That is, as the African centered movement developed it was reflected in the cultural product which included rap music. This "new awareness" fused with nationalism would become transformative. "This Afrocentrism could then infuse the best image [sic] and interests of Black people into popular culture and allow it to fuse into a liberating national culture."[36]

As Afrocentrism was challenged in academic circles and a backlash redeveloped within America, the basic ideology of African centeredness remained but the imagery and culture products which symbolized adherence and advocacy to its philosophy waned. Simultaneously, the burgeoning political climate within rap was replaced by materialist and gangsta rap culture.

Ultimately images of group unity were replaced with a less useful form of group unity, gangs. Seemingly, rap reverted to the very institutions from which youth elevated themselves to form HC. Consequently, the battle for the future of HC waged between and among the black community activist, corporate interest and producers of the art is more fervent than at any other time in its brief history. What is missing from conceptualizing HC within Black Nationalism's ideology is that ownership of modes and medium which delivered the "best image and interest of Black people into popular culture" remains the property of those viewed as the historical adversary of African people. Tricia Rose captures the crux of the matter. Rose does not believe, as many Black Nationalists do, that resistance to hegemonic dominance can occur solely outside of market culture. Rose believes that resistance can and must take place not only outside of market culture but inside commodified spaces. Her position is worth repeating for it highlights the challenge to HC and Black Nationalism in its attempt to magnify its political positions via the very formations and agencies it distrust and despise. Rose remarks:

> Commodified cultural production is a deeply *dangerous but crucial* terrain for developing politically progressive expression at this historical moment. In other words whatever counterhegemonic work is

done outside the market, work that takes place inside
it is also very important. In a way inside and outside
are fictitious, since market forces and market logic to
one degree or another pervade all American culture
and politics.[37]

Rose identifies the great difficulty in attempting to manipulate market-based culture politics from below: a point which is
not lost when one considers that the ownership of the modes
of communication is usually in the hands of politically detached
ownership. For instance, of the major Hip Hop journals and
magazines, only one, *Rap Sheet*, is owned and published by an
African-American, Darryl James.[38] In a phone interview, James
suggested that the major hurdle for self ownership of such media
was the lack of vision of the people thus served. Ultimately while
Black Nationalism is a useful tool of analyzing HC, it must
include more emphasis on ownership of the agencies responsible
for broadcasting the culture's aspirations through its product
since this area presents HC's greatest challenge. This represents
a clear indication that those categories of the pre-scientific stage
articulated by Jones have not been realized. Thus, HC remains
in a war without weapons of theory.

Houston Baker's text, *Black Studies, Rap and the Academy*
seem to be a step in the right direction. Baker attempts to highlight the responsibility of the academy to connect with popular
culture. Baker focuses on rap's "hybridity" to illustrate that its
content and context is historically universal and not parochial. As
a result of such universality, the academy has a duty to adequately
incorporate rap as pedagogy and more importantly, as a subject
of research. However, a more useful "universalist" approach
would insist that all the elements of HC, which encompasses
rap, should be the focus of academic work.

A favorable critique articulates the responsibility of academe
to the postmodern black experience advanced by Baker as an
imperative.[39] A less favorable critique describes Baker's work as
detached scholarship rooted in academic arrogance.[40] The fear is
that bourgeois elitism would undermine, co-opt and neutralize
grassroots political activism that Rose identifies as emanating
"from below." Baker sometimes gives legitimacy to such criti-

cism. For instance, on one occasion, he suggests that Henry V and William Shakespeare were both "rappers."[41] Thus using the rap format presented in their work makes it easier to comprehend their contributions. Using rap as a tool to advance studies regarding the culture of the West is unimpressive and contributes little to advance the interests of HC. Nevertheless, both critiques are accepted for both to provide some accurate description of Baker's work. The former yields a more useful function. Debates regarding authenticity, politics, and cultural value must occur within academic circles as well as grassroots circles. The literature regarding post industrialism and HC offers evidence of the need for a connection between the academy and HC.

Post Industrial Politics and Hip Hop Culture

The second frame of reference for understanding the complexities of HC is conceptualized within an area of study referred to as "Post Industrialism." Post industrialism encompasses the changing urban landscape due to gentrification, the loss of manufacturing, unequal access to education/job training, changing immigration patterns, and the shift of industry to a technology base. Economist John Kain in 1968, and later John Kasarda, developed the *Spacial Mismatch Theory* which gives a more detailed scenario. The theory proposed that joblessness increased as manufacturing jobs decreased. Policy decisions, such as denying mass transit to the suburban areas, resulted in diminished accessibility to jobs in those areas at a time when many industries were locating there. In addition, the economy shifted from a market economy to a service economy. Jobs shifted to rural, suburban areas and overseas. Job skills for black city residents did not match job requirements, hence a mismatch was created. Concurrently, the number of blacks in cities increased as gentrification occurred. The black population, especially males, would suffer the most as a result of under education, underdeveloped employment and social skills and the reluctance of industry to locate within the city limits.[42]

The seminal discussion regarding post industrialism which encompasses HC is presented by Tricia Rose. Rose demonstrates how adverse city policies responding to these realities disrupted black urban life, thereby leading to underdevelopment, the creation of slums and the rise of poverty. This is especially true of urban centers in the north, like New York. Her research revealed that,

> Between the late 1930s and late 1960s [Robert] Moses, a very powerful city planner, executed a number of public works projects, highways parks, and housing projects which significantly reshaped the profile of New York City. In 1959, Robert Moses began construction of the Cross-Bronx Expressway which would cut directly through the center of the most heavily populated working class areas in the Bronx. While he could have modified his route slightly to bypass densely populated working-class ethnic residential communities, he elected a path that required the demolition of 159 buildings. Throughout the 1960s and early 1970s, some 60,000 Bronxite's homes were razed. Designating these old blue collar housing units as "slums," Moses's Title I Slum Clearance Program forced the relocation of 170,000 people.[43]

These numbers increased as landlords sold their property to avoid financial loss resulting from depreciation of property. Simultaneously, city government cut thousands of jobs in an attempt to avoid bankruptcy. President Gerald Ford vetoed a loan bailout request by the city which led to budget cuts.[44] These budget cuts adversely affected social services which added to the devastation of the city's residents. The connection here is that these very communities would be responsible for the creation of HC, especially its most politicized forms.[45]

Elsewhere, Rose frames her discussion of the politics of HC within the context of the use of "public space." Public space includes concert venues where permits, high insurance and fear of black people in general often lead to denied access of youth to gather. Rose presents the deliberate tactics of government agencies, politicians and media who effectively deny rap music public space to address what she sees as the move towards public censorship of HC. Rose believes that this censorship is an attempt to undermine HC's viability as a political force. In her words,

> Rap's poetic voice is deeply political in content and spirit, community responses, and the interpretation of black expression constitutes rap's hidden politics; hegemonic discourses have rendered these institutional aspects of black cultural politics invisible. Political interpretations of rap's explosive and resistive lyrics are critical to understanding contemporary black cultural politics, but reflect only part of the battle. Rap's hidden politics must also be revealed and contested; otherwise, whether we believe the hype or not won't make a difference.[46]

Robin D. G. Kelley elaborates on the issue of public space. Similar to Rose, it is located within the context of post industrialism. He writes,

> The simultaneous decline in employment opportunities; public leisure spaces for young people; and overly crowded, poorly funded public schools and youth programs simply expanded an urban landscape in which black teenagers--the throwaways of a new, mobile capitalism--became an even larger, more permanent (and in the minds of many, more menacing) presence in parks and on street corners.[47]

Art as politics and ultimately HC must be viewed as a response to a continuum of unequal labor relationships where production value, social meaning and profit interact. Attempts to provide counter-hegemonic avenues are intertwined with the reality that many of its producers (African youth) must out of necessity respond to earning wages as a condition to simply exist in a society where wages determine the nature of your existence. Kelley states that urban youth have responded to dire circumstances and carved spaces for themselves through the commodification of *play*, termed "play labor." He states,

> The growing numbers of young brown bodies engaged in "play" rather than work...have contributed to the popular constructions of the "underclass" as a threat and shaped urban police practices.[48]

The altered creative expression of urban youth led to the production of a variety of culture forms to which Hip Hop culture belongs. Kelley warns that he is not presenting self commodification as emancipatory, revolutionary or even resistive.[49] The point, however, is that

> Capitalism has become both their greatest friend and greatest foe. It has the capacity to create spaces for their entrepreneurial imaginations and their symbolic work to allow them to turn something for a profit, and to permit them to hone their skills and imagine getting paid.[50]

In addition, rather than try to change the person through rigid regimentation . . . . we need to change the streets themselves, the built environment, the economy, and the racist discourse that dominates popular perceptions of black youth.[51]

Nelson George, described by many as an authority regarding the social, political and economic impact of black music in America,[52] presents arguably the most comprehensive book to date regarding HC. George presents an insider's analysis while effectively demonstrating the sociological consequences of postindustrialism and how they shaped HC. He argues that, "the federal government under President Nixon cut back on Democratic anti poverty programs and systematically ignored the economic development pleas of America's urbanites, whose jobs were fleeing to the suburbs."[53]

This in part led to the formation of a drug economy in many urban centers which arrested the development of many African youth. George believes that the availability of drugs starting with heroin, could not have been possible "without widespread police and political corruption aiding in its dissemination."[54] Currently the most devastating of these illicit drugs is crack cocaine. According to George:

> The crack industry became able employers of teenagers, filling the economic vacuum created by the ongoing loss of working-class jobs to the suburbs and then to poor Third World countries. Teenagers and adolescents were zealously recruited to provide the

unskilled labor needed for manufacturing, packaging and selling illegal drugs. By 1992 it was estimated that as many as 150, 000 people were employed in New York City's drug trade. Similarly large numbers could be found in most major cities.[55]

The effects sent a ripple effect throughout many African communities: A point which is not lost when one examines the rise of the prison industrial complex, the incarceration rates of African males, and the profits to private corporations from this nation's heavy investment in prison and African prisoners. One unfortunate irony is that at times HC seems to celebrate its nihilism, a point that its adversaries quickly emphasize. Bakari Kitwana accurately describes the paradox. He states, "Often highlighted are those aspects of rap which, despite their seemingly anti establishment, angry and street life presentations do not threaten the status quo, (2) reinforce negative stereotypes about Blacks, (3) manipulate these stereotypes to increase sales, and (4) move rap music further away from its grassroots origins."[56]

Discourse on post industrialism offers an opportunity for aspects of HC to be examined as a consequence of the American political system. Frameworks developed to address the needs of African people as they seek power offer HC its greatest challenge. The issue that confronts HC confronts African people generally. Consequently, theories and methodologies that attempt to prescribe remedies for the African predicament are also applicable to HC. Ultimately three predominant paradigms serve such an essential purpose. They represent the future of social science inquiry regarding HC.

Another apparent example of this void pertains to religion as a viable instrument within HC. The lack of an attempt to locate HC within one of African people's most important institutions reflects the void. Consequently, the literature is scarce. There are, however, a few chapters written on the subject, but the majority connect HC's politicized ideals to Islam, to be specific, African-American Islam.[57] Eric Perkins Williams' "Nation of Islam Ideology in the Rap of Public Enemy" identifies the stages of politicized rap discussed previously. He refers to politicized rap as message rap.

The latest stage has been rap laced with religious ideology that emanates from the Nation of Islam. Public Enemy has provided a medium through which the NOI's eschatology and worldview is articulated.[58]

Angela Spense Nelson's essay presents a useful but incomplete assessment of HC and religious ideology.[59] Rapper Kool Moe Dee and Public Enemy's worldview are described as religious. The worldview and religious ideologies of both artists are represented and discussed as theological contributors to HC, and its political viability is severely questioned. Kool Moe Dee is an artist whose contributions are rife with social commentary, moral instructions and positive messages, but they do not qualify him to be placed in the same context as Public Enemy. While Kool Moe Dee does have a few lines in his songs that express the positive utility of reading the Bible and Koran and turning to God,[60] the majority of his contributions rests in social commentary which is not explicitly religious. A more useful essay that connects HC to organized politicized religious doctrine is provided by Ernest Allen jr. His article, "Making the Strong Survive: The Contours and Contradictions of Message Rap,"[61] successfully presents the earliest manifestation of religious ideology within HC.

The Nation of Islam and the Five Percenters, presently referred to as the Nation of Gods and Earths (NGE), developed these agencies that aided in the development of a politicized theology. Allen traces the theology and describes the eschatology and worldview of both. Consequent to describing the doctrine, Allen identifies artists who articulate these views. This approach is much more empirically sound and represents a more useful scholarship regarding religion as a viable political instrument of HC.[62]

Article critic, Harry Allen, a writer for HC periodicals such as *VIBE* and *The Source*, was among the first to offer literature regarding the Nation of Gods and Earth and their contribution to HC. Allen's article titled "Righteous Indignation" exposes artists affiliated with Islam and their influence of HC.[63] These periodicals are the most valuable writings on this interaction between theology and HC because they present the recurring problem resulting from the vacuum between HC and the academy. No serious attempt is made to develop a definitive method of determining whether HC has a political philosophy rooted in religious theology, by what means do we identify it and what considerations should be made to determine its viability. Such a void once again demonstrates the urgency to investigate the political viability of HC and justifies the need for this book to be written.

Hip Hop as Art

In summary, much of the literature written on HC not developed within the frameworks discussed presents it in the context of art. Literature focuses on the personalities and biographies that shape the culture. Content that reflects some semblance of political activity is usually accompanied with sensationalism, exploitative business practices, unequal distribution of income within the industry, internal squabbles, and rumor. Such books include but are not limited to, *Gangsta: Merchandising the Rhymes of Violence* and *Have Gun Will Travel : The Spectacular Rise and Violent Fall of Death Row Records:* by Ronin Ro, *Fight the Power* by Chuck D of Public Enemy, *No Disrespect* by Sista Souljah, a stream of books about the late TuPac Shakur, LL Cool J's *I make My Own Rules*, Queen Latifah's *Ladies First: Revelations from a Strong Woman* and a host of others.

Understandably with its market appeal, all sorts of merchandise marketed to youth culture have "Hip Hop" in their brand title. It reminds one of the market fervor attached to Afrocentrism. We experienced Afrocentric bibles, learning tools for children, wedding gifts, home decorations, churches, schools, etc. A reminder that even reputed emancipatory philosophies can be co-opted by the market place. Recently, HC has experienced a similar fate. There is a Hip Hop bible, dictionaries, learning tools for children such as *Addition: Rap Version (Rock 'N Learn)*, *Division (Rap With the Facts Series)* and a host of instruction learning tools. The term "hip hop," used to target youth is connected to a variety of consumer goods and the list is growing daily.

Other texts written by authors labeled as insiders usually attempt to address an array of issues not limited to HC. HC is not central to their overall assessment of contemporary America but its impact is undeniable. The most cited of these is written by Greg Tate.[64] Tate grapples with issues from the changing philosophy of Amiri Baraka, criticism of Henry Louis Gates, Hip Hop politics, the death of the Harlem Renaissance, and media to name a few.

David Toop, author of one of the earliest books written on Rap culture,[65] presents the genesis of rap in an encyclopedic form detailed with vintage photographs of rap's pioneers during late seventies and early eighties. The personal accounts of many artists leave the reader with a greater sense of the social, political and economic challenges that contributed to or impeded the development of HC. Toop identifies graffiti artists, breakers, rappers and DJ's who were instrumental contributors. Sadly and consistent with many African-American progenitors of incorporated popular forms of black music, many are forgotten and only recently have the magnitude of their contributions been acknowledged. Thus, these works are worthy of mention for they represent the first wave of scholarship that is necessary. The awareness and centrality of HC would not have been possible without contributions of these writers who attempt to locate it within the spectrum of art, politics and, social relevance. The contemporary challenge is to locate HC within the sphere of a relevant social science where investigatory practices do not merely mimic an irrelevant worldview, but seek the development of new paradigms.

There must be an expectation that if judgments about the political nature of HC are made, such evaluations should be made by political scientists and political science using political constructs. Although not political scientists in political science are qualified to make judgments about HC's political elements, one would expect much more analyses with political orientations to subsist within the body of literature. Such orientations are lacking. The addition is necessary if the intent is to distinguish between HC's positive and negative elements where recommendations regarding its political utility are made. In addition, standards, parameters and a structural apparatus such as the constituent elements of a political philosophy allow us to make sound decisions devoid of emotionalism and editorializing about what the functions of HC *are* and ought to be from a political science perspective.

Chapter III
BLACK THEOLOGY
AND HIP HOP CULTURE

Historically, many of the strategies and philosophies that have informed the African-American struggle for freedom and justice in America have been grounded in religious doctrines. Whether it was used as a tool to control the enslaved, a revolutionary creed to support slave insurrections, a catechism to provide moral suasion for abolitionist or a manifesto to give ideological and moral justification for the civil rights movement, the centrality of religion as a political instrument in this struggle is incontrovertible. Politics and religion have been inseparable forces in the African-American odyssey. This chapter examines the relationship between HC and religious doctrines to determine the extent to which HC embodies a political philosophy and, to the extent to which evidence of a philosophy is apparent we attempt to assess its viability.

Given the fact that in the popular media HC is frequently discussed as a morally degenerate art form driven by values and an ethic that run counter to dominant Christian principles, some may be surprised with this line of inquiry. However, research reveals that HC as rebel culture operates within the paradigm of the historical connection of religion, politics and the struggle for liberation. HC's resistance to traditional Christian ideology does not mean that it is bereft of a religious foundation. Rather it signifies only that it is grounded in a different theology, a theology that confronts and in many instances contradicts traditional Christian teachings and at times ridicules them.

The data shows that much of HC is conditioned by the religious ideas and teaching of the Nation of Islam (NOI) and the Nation of Gods and Earths (NGE) and that these ideas constitute a distinct political philosophy. The ideas of these two groups are interwoven in the lyrical content of HC and many of the artists have or have had political connections to organizations and personalities affiliated with NOI or NGE. Examining the evolution of HC and major HC groups and personalities and the content of their works to demonstrate their religious connections and the nature of their political philosophies, I must first convey what I mean by a viable political philosophy.

According to Mills, a political philosophy includes theories that explain the nature and origins of political society, statements of goals to be pursued, identification of institutions or agencies through which they are to be pursued and ideological precepts to be used in mobilizing and exhorting adherents to action. Building on Mills, Jones has argued that political philosophies contain five distinct constituent elements: theories, statement of ideals, identification of historical agencies, ideology, and ethical standards for evaluating people and the institutions they create. As Jones states:

> Taken together, as an integrated philosophy, these elements provide a basis for interpreting, political reality, prescribing the desired future, determining what practices and institutions would be the appropriate structures for pursuing that future, and for evaluating the people and the institutions involved in the enterprise[66]

The constituent elements can help to delineate the political philosophy embodied in the NOI and NGE and demonstrate how it is reflected in the lyrics and overall culture of Hip Hop.

Black Theology, Political Philosophy and the Evolution of Hip Hop

A black liberating theology as summarized by Maulana Karenga,

> is centered around several core contentions that appear in varying and similar forms in most writings

Figure 1. African-American Islamic Groups

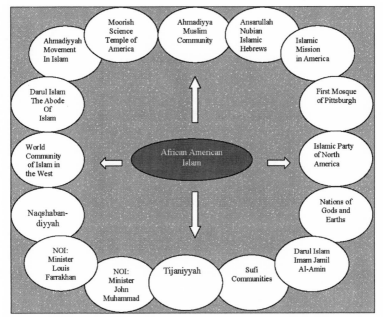

on it. Among these are: (1) the need for a God in Black people's own image and interest, i.e., Black and of and for the ppressed; (2) the imperative that religion must reflect the interests of Blacks and concretely and actively benefit them; (3) the contention that Blacks are a "chosen people" or "covenant community" i.e., have a special relationship with God; (4) the recognition of the Black Church's radical history and a call for its resuming this role in the liberation struggle of Black people; and (5) the indispensability of social struggle to liberate Blacks–socially and spiritually–and realize God's will to bring truth, freedom, and justice to society and the world.[67]

These core contentions are found throughout HC. Its political philosophy is extracted from the nationalism and black liberation theology of the NOI and the NGE. The black liberation theology that emanates from the NOI and NGE is embedded in the fabric of HC.

Islam as practiced by African-Americans has been the subject of much controversy. Much of the controversy centers on questions regarding the extent to which Islam as practiced by African-Americans conforms to traditional Islamic laws and customs. It is commonly agreed that the NOI, the most widely known Islamic sect in African-American communities, departs in significant ways from more orthodox Islam. As demonstrated by figure 1, there are numerous other Islamic groups in America,[68] but most HC groups subscribe in varying degrees to the precepts of the NOI and its progeny, the NGE. Accordingly, the political philosophy of HC is derived from the doctrine of these two organizations.

Louis E. Lomax, a Malcolm X biographer, who highlights areas of contention between traditional Islam and African-American Islam argued that the major point of contention is that orthodox Moslems condemn the Black Muslim teaching that the white man is the devil. The ideal of a black separate state is also a point of disagreement between traditional Islam and African-American Islam.

Though Lomax is specifically describing the Nation of Islam (NOI) as it existed prior to the 1960, his insight applies to many African-American factions of Islam, but there are a few exceptions. Relatively few sects have reformulated their practices to align with orthodox customs. The NOI, under the leadership of Wallace D. Muhammad, represents one such exception. According to Clifton E. Marsh,

> Wallace, in his role as spiritual leader, has managed to alter the doctrine of the former "Black Muslims." These changes enabled the Word Community of Al-Islam in the West to be accepted by the United States government. The organization is no longer considered a threat to internal security.[69]

Hip Hop as a counter culture embraces Islam and rejects Christianity, the unofficial state religion. The overwhelming acceptance of Islam is in part based on HC's identity with the oppressed and the perception of Islam as a force that confronts imperialism, western arrogance and cultural hegemony. Whether this is an accurate characterization of Islam is not the central issue here. The reality is that many youth within HC perceive it as radical and adversarial, two essential qualities of the HC.

The Nation of Islam

The Nation of Islam was founded by Master Wali Fard Muhammad, who according to doctrine, is the long awaited *Mahdi* or messiah of black people in North America. His mission was to spread the knowledge of Islam among African-Americans in Detroit, Michigan in the 1930s. Wali Fard Muhammad's primary focus is characterized by its ethical emphasis or "man's ability to correct man."[70] Self-respect and self-reliance are at the core of his teachings. This period marked an important turning point in the lives of African-Americans due in part to the economic severity of the depression as well as the vast number of blacks migrating to the north seeking relief from social, economic and legal disfranchisement in the south. Master Fard's teachings were accepted by many Africans in America and within a relatively short period of time, many accepted the religion as a method of reaffirming themselves as dignified human beings worthy of love and respect. Master Fard's teachings attracted many followers, among them The Honorable Elijah Muhammad, who adopted aspects of the religion of Islam to form the Nation of Islam.

While serving time in prison, Malcolm Little, later identified as Malcolm X, accepted NOI doctrine. Upon Malcolm's release, The Nation of Islam had one of its most charismatic leaders. Through the efforts of Elijah Muhammad, Malcolm X and others, the faith spread from Detroit to Chicago and eventually touched every major American city, as well as a few Caribbean countries. With the death of Elijah Muhammad in 1975 and the departure of Malcolm X, the Nation of Islam would be fragmented and several different groups evolved. The Nation of Islam under the leadership of John Muhammad and Louis Farrakhan maintained and spread the doctrine professed by Elijah Muhammad from 1975 to the present (See figure 2).

Figure 2. Nation of Islam Groups

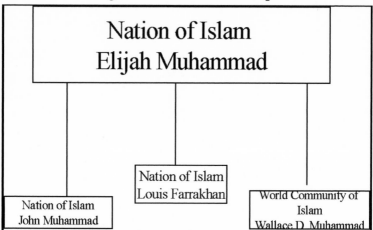

The Nation of Gods and Earths and Father Allah

The Nation of Gods and Earths emerged from the teachings of the NOI. The NGE'score belief was that the "Blackman" was divine and despite the social, economic and, political trauma blacks continue to experience, they would resurrect a proud self-reliant nation in North America.

Clarence 13X, the founder of NGE, otherwise known as Father Allah, used the doctrines of the NOI as the core of NGE ideology. It is important to include some of his biographical information in this research for it partly explains the development of a relationship between HC and NGE theology and demonstrates the incorporation of NOI ideology within the NGE. One member offers a useful insight:

> Father Allah and Justice left Nation of Islam Temple #7 and delivered the Truth to the people whom they felt needed it most, the young people in the streets of Harlem. They delivered their Universal message by word of mouth with the knowledge that its power would transcend the barriers that typically hinder oral communication. As word of their teaching spread, more young blacks sought them out to discover the truth. The truth was manifested to each student through the knowledge of themselves and their original culture. Prior to receiving proper

> education, the first born students were street hustlers
> and thugs, as was the Father during a brief period in
> his life. As each student was educated, he began to
> refine his words, ways and actions in order to reflect
> righteousness and freedom.[71]

Clarence 13X was born Clarence Smith on February 22, 1928, in segregated Danville, Virginia. His mother moved to New York in the early 1940s and Clarence followed in 1946. In 1950 he joined the Army, served for three years and consequently fought in the Korean War. Upon his return to America and finding that his wife had joined The Nation of Islam, he too joined and spent the next 42 months in Mosque #7 in Harlem, the mosque led by Minister Malcolm X. During this time, Clarence 13X was able to move up through the ranks to become a lieutenant in The Fruit of Islam (FOI), which served as a symbolic military wing of the organization. Their main function was to protect members of The Nation of Islam and keep order in the community. Clarence 13X trained members in military tactics and skills which he acquired while in the military. During this era, the NOI grew rapidly. Some say that the growth was based on the charismatic leadership of Malcolm X, while others believe that it resulted from the political climate which provided few alternatives for black men. The NOI spread rapidly over the next several years. Temples were formed nationwide, but the headquarters remained in Chicago under the leadership of Elijah Muhammad.

In 1963, Clarence 13X was expelled from the NOI. There is discrepancy regarding the reason for his dismissal. One newspaper published by his followers, titled *The Word*, indicated that some of the contemporaries of Clarence 13X reported that marital problems, his love for gambling and conflict with NOI doctrine may have all contributed to his departure.[72] Another writer believes that the time of his departure from the organization is still open to debate.[73]

According to Ernest Allen:

> Legend has it that he was expelled from NOI Temple
> No. 7 by Malcolm X, which would place his depar-
> ture prior to December. Complicating the story,

however, are FBI reports stating that Clarence 13X
consistently attended New York City NOI affairs
from1963 through March 1965.[74]

In May of 1965 Clarence 13X, speaking in front of Hotel
Theresa, was arrested for unlawful assembly and disorderly
conduct. With such a controversial worldview and ontology, it
would be safe to assume that the end of the movement was near.
In fact the reverse happened. Upon his release, the movement
gained momentum and grew rapidly in New York, New Jersey
and in various prisons including the infamous Rikers Island.
When Clarence 13X departed from the NOI, he took with him
what Earnest Allen calls "internally transmitted catechisms."
According to Allen, these "Would provide the basis for the
emergence of a new Islamic nationalist movement destined to
take hold among scores of African youth a quarter century later."
An account of such an emergence is reflected in HC's adherence
to the philosophy of the NGE. A detailed examination of the
cosmogony of the NGE clearly demonstrates that Clarence 13X
utilized the teachings of the Honorable Elijah Muhammad. While
the similarities are obvious, there are some differences. The NGE
reject the labels of "religion" and "Muslim" while simultaneously
embracing the teachings of Master Fard, who is said to have
traveled from Mecca to spread the knowledge of Islam to Blacks
in the United States. Their rejection of these labels reflects the
attempt to be distinguished from what is considered traditional
Islam. According to several interviewees, their word and practice
are one, thus reflecting a way of life not a religion.

While Clarence 13 X left the Nation of Islam in part because
of divergent ontological issues, the NGE considers *The Story of
Master Fard* and *Message to the Blackman*, both by Elijah Muhammad, to be the most important books after the Holy Qur'an.

Post Industrialism, the NOI, NGE and the Emergence of HC

As described in Chapter II, post industrialism encompasses
the changing urban landscape due to gentrification, the loss of
manufacturing, unequal access to education/job training, changing immigration patterns and the shift of industry to a technology

base. The neighborhoods where most of the Hip Hop pioneers such as Grandmaster Flash, Kool Herc, and Afrika Bambaataa lived were neighborhoods hardest hit by post industrialism. A clear connection between HC, NOI, NGE and post industrialism was established. Names such as Scientific, Born, Supreme, Divine, Infinite and a host of others that reflect affiliation with the NGE decorated apartment buildings and were frequently mentioned on radio call in programs.[75] Youth who actively converted to NGE and NOI were also affiliates of HC. Conversion to these doctrines was common in the early 1980s as HC grew. Their philosophy provided explanations for the dire circumstances that many inner city youth experienced as involuntary participants and victims of urbanization. Urban renewal projects, the flight of manufacturing industries from the city to the perimeters of New Jersey and New York State, new immigrant laborers and the perceived absence of a black political agenda all contributed in shaping such a hostile environment.[76] It is hardly a coincidence that politicized HC emanated from these neighborhoods. It is also beyond coincidence that these neighborhoods were incubators for recruits for both NOI and NGE.

Consequently, the overwhelming majority of politicized HC comes from these marginalized communities.[77] The two organizations helped shape the worldview of the majority of youth in these communities where formal Christianity failed to articulate their frustration. "Five Percenters" doctrines reflect an impatience with the Black church; a position that the majority of youth, especially those supporters of HC accept. Praying to a "mystery God" to solve the problems caused by the historical enemy of the "Blackman" was considered shortsighted and bordered on suicide. It was considered equivalent to Native Americans performing the "Ghost Dance" which would evoke spirits who would ultimately save them from their slaughter. Their prayers were unanswered. As a result, African youth identified with the more radical doctrines of both organizations. The reputed founders of HC themselves were confronted with choosing between competing political ideologies of Christianity and Islam. Most chose the latter. The worldview of the early pioneers of HC was molded by the urban dilemmas referenced as well as the solutions offered by non Christian religious communities. As an adolescent, Afrika Bambaataa recalls,

> I was watching all of that and then later when gangs were fading out I decided to get into the Nation of Islam. It brought about a big change on me. It got me to respect people even though they might not like us because we was [sic] Muslim. The Nation of Islam was doing things that America had been trying to for a while, taking people from the streets like junkies and prostitutes and cleaning them up. Rehabilitating them like the jail system was not doing.[78]

The changing of Bambaataa's worldview from gang member to member of Nation of Islam would be central to the development of one of the most important organizations within HC, The Zulu Nation. A group of youth in the Bronx started a small organization called the Zulu Kings through which they attempted to connect themselves to African spiritual ancestry through deed and dress, including beads and other forms of African jewelry. The name later changed to the Zulu Nation as involvement from youth in other communities in New York increased. The organization would spread to Los Angeles through another HC pioneer, Africa Islam. He recalls, "I invented the chapters, the councils, and started structuring the military formations of all the Zulu chapters that were around. So I was like the Malcolm X if Africa Bambaataa was Elijah Muhammad."[79]

The group stressed many of the same tenets of the Nation of Islam and The Five Percent Nation. Taking pride in one's heritage, family, community and self-sufficiency is among these tenets. Violent confrontation between groups in different groups in different neighborhoods diminished and was replaced with competition between DJs and MCs (rappers). The winner would claim supremacy and neighborhood youth would support their sound systems and travel with them as they "battle" other crews. While this may seem somewhat trivial, it represented the single most effective method through which HC spread and its political ideas germinated within urban communities.

Political Theory, NOI, NGE and HC

As noted, a political philosophy includes a theory about the nature, origin and conflicts of society. Specifically a theory includes a vision of the origin of society and government, the nature and purpose of the state, the major forces in society and their relationship with each other, the major societal conflicts and the range of acceptable solutions to these conflicts and, the major problems facing the group.[80] Yet some theories that emanate from the theology of the NOI and NGE are reflected in HC as evidence of a political philosophy. All of the elements which comprise a theory are found in NOI doctrine. Regarding the nature and origin of the state, according to NOI doctrine the white man is a grafted genetic creation of the original "Blackman." Similar to the NOI, the NGE believe that, "the original man, Allah has declared, is none other than the Blackman. The Blackman is the first and the last, maker and owner of the universe. From him came all brown, yellow, red and white people."[81]

This mythology is the foundation of a view that professes the divinity of the "Blackman" which is central to both NOI and NGE doctrine and found throughout HC.[82] The American state government and its institutions, according to NOI and NGE, came into being to advance the interest of Europeans in America. Many members within HC express similar sentiment. This is especially true regarding their views on law enforcement, politicians and the American educational system. As one lyricist puts it,

> You have the emergence in human society of this
> thing that's called the State.
> What is the State?
> The State is this organized bureaucracy.
> It is the police department. It is the Army, the
> Navy.
> It is the prison system, the courts, and what have you.
> This is the State—it is a repressive organization.
> You'd be killing each other if there were no police!
> But the reality is the police become necessary in
> human society only at that

Figures 3 and 4. Pin and Flag of the NGE

Junction in human history where there is a split
      between those who have and
Those who ain't got.[83]

The theory of both NOI and NGE concerning the major
problems of American society is closely related to their position
on the nature and/or origin of the state. They argue that belief
in black inferiority by many segments of the population, a slave
mentality of many blacks, the belief in white supremacy, and the
presence of crime, drugs and poverty in black neighborhoods
constitute major societal problems. Such problems according to
the theory are sustained by the educational system, corporate
structures, and America's social institutions. According to both
groups, these problems can be solved after Africans in America
gain "knowledge of self." By knowledge of self the NOI means
the process through which blacks gain a sense of their history
and heritage, become economically self sufficient and gain a
complete understanding of God. Elijah Muhammad explains
this in his major treatise, *Message to the Blackman.* The connection between HC and the teachings of Elijah Muhammad
is readily apparent. Scores of artists, especially those considered
political lyricists, express the need for "knowledge of self."[84] In
addition, the image of Elijah Muhammad was visible in several
rap videos. Other symbols associated with NOI and the NGE
that are highly visible within HC during this period included the

star and crescent, the flag of the NOI and the flag of the NGE (depicted in figures 3 and 4), Muhammad *Speaks* newspapers, Malcolm X speeches, the *X* symbol which denotes loss of cultural identity and random footage of the Fruits of Islam.

Also, hundreds of artists infused the teachings of Elijah Muhammad into their lyrics. A few artists paid tribute by naming their albums according to some teachings of the NOI.[85] Another corresponding theory is located within a doctrine that concurrently identifies the major forces in society and their relationship to each other and is central to both NGE and NOI philosophy. This component of a theory is explained in a pamphlet titled "Lost Found Lesson No. 2," written by W. D. Fard, founder of the Nation of Islam. It is reprinted by Ernest Allen.

14. Question: Who is the 85%?

Answer: The uncivilized people, poison animal eaters, slaves from mental death and death power. People who do not know the living god or their origin in this world and they worship that they know not what, and who are easily led in the wrong direction but hard to lead in the right direction.

15. Question: Who is the 10 %?

Answer: The rich, the slave makers of the poor, who teach the poor lies to believe that the almighty true and living god is a spook and cannot be seen with the physical eye. Otherwise known as the bloodsuckers of the poor.

16. Question: Who is the 5% on this poor part of the earth?

Answer: They are the poor, righteous teachers who do not believe in the teaching of the 10% and are all wise and know who the living god is and teach that the living god is the Son of Man, the supreme being, the black man from Asia; and teach freedom, justice and equality to all the human families of the planet earth, otherwise known as civilized people, also as Moslem and Moslem sons.[86]

While HC has adopted what may be called the more radical element of the NOI's depiction of the problems confronting blacks and proposed solutions to them, HC has not adopted the more moderate descriptions and solutions endorsed by the NOI. Proposals to address the problems by reducing the high school drop out rate, creating jobs, and participating in local politics are virtually ignored by HC.[87]

HC's appeal to youth is not found in such remedies but in harsh criticism of black politicians, assertions about the wickedness of America, predictions about the coming apocalypse (for whites only), and exalted self esteem reflected in the divination of the "Blackman." These themes are reflected within HC and represent the foundation on which HC's political philosophy rests.

Statement of Ideals, the NOI, NGE and HC

Statement of ideals identify broad transcendental goals to be pursued.[88] The purpose of this section is to identify whether statements of ideals contained in NOI and NGE theology are adopted by HC. Taken together with the other constituent elements, the existence of statements of ideals within HC would be further evidence of a political philosophy.

The ideals of the NOI are expressed under the heading of "What the Muslim Wants" in the *Muslim Program*, written by Elijah Muhammad that appears in every edition of the *Muhammad Speaks*. The ideals include the desire for a separate state or territory, equality of opportunity, the immediate end to police brutality, separate and equal education, exemption from taxation and equal justice under the law. The NGE accepts such ideals and believes that they can be advanced once certain "lessons" are accepted. These lessons, drawn from the teaching of the NOI and referred to as "120 degrees of knowledge," include:

1. The Twelve Jewels of Islam
2. Supreme Mathematics
3. Lost and Found Muslim Lesson # 1 (1-10)
4. Student Enrollment (1-10)
5. Breakdown of the Enrollment (1-10)
6. One to Thirty-six
7. Applied Mathematics of the Actual Facts
8. Lost and Found Muslim Lesson #2 (1-40)
9. Solar Facts
10. Actual Facts
11. Allah World Manifested
12. Four Directions

13.   Power and Refinement
14.   5% or the Stages of the Mind
15.   Five credits of a Black Woman
16.   Six rules of the Black Woman
17.   Allah–360%
18.   Seven Prophets of Allah
19.   General Muk Muk's History
20.   The Hog[89]

Hip Hop artists often cite these lessons in many of their songs. Most notable is a group known as Brand Nubian, whose members describe themselves as dutiful warriors spreading the word to liberate the 85% with this worldview. Their albums are saturated with lessons, including the "Twelve Jewels and "The 120."[90]

What must be interjected here is that these artists are not marginal artists operating on the periphery of HC. They are legitimized by their peers, general HC, African youth in various communities and, one of the most important aspects of HC, the underground. Thus, their political philosophy reaches a wide audience potentially shaping their normative ideas, a central component in the development of a worldview. The following verse expresses the prevailing view.

> The knowledge, is, the foundation
> The wisdom is the way
> The understanding shows you
> That you are on your way
> The culture is our God
> The power is the truth
> Equality only shows you
> That you have planted your roots
> God came to teach us of the righteous way
> How to build and be born
> On this glorious day
> The knowledge of the cipher is
> To enlighten you
> That God is right beside you.[91]

Reflected throughout much of HC, this view is especially prominent in the language of other artists such as Kam and Paris, who have direct links to the NOI as informal ambassadors.

Underlying the ideals expressed in a political philosophy is some conception of the good life. The good life as expressed in HC is not always consistent with the ideals in the doctrine imported from the NOI and the NGE. A careful analysis reveals that HC postulates four distinct avenues through which the good life may be achieved. They are materialism, religious advocacy, cultural awareness and what I have chosen to call didactic nihilism. Materialism, as it appears in HC, holds that gaining wealth by any means necessary actualizes the good life. Expressions of narcissism and braggadocio are pervasive. Scolding those who have attempted to gain wealth but failed is a major concern.[92] Religious advocacy, as it appears in HC, holds the good life is achieved by adhering to religious principles and doctrine. Principles and doctrines produced by the NOI and the NGE are most prevalent. Culture awareness, as it appears in HC, holds that the good life is achieved by acknowledging one's culture and history.

Acknowledgment and acceptance lead to black nationalism, political, economic, and social cooperation and ultimately a Black utopia.[93] Didactic nihilism, as expressed in HC, holds that the good life is achieved by learning and participating in every possible vice. This term describes aspects of HC that reinforce undesirable behavior by instructing its listeners on the best methods to accomplish such.[94] A few verses from the artist known as the Notorious B. I. G dramatizes the point. He instructs his audience on the ten rules of crack manufacturing and distribution. According to his commands,

> Number three: never trust no-bo-dy
> Your moms'll set that *ss up, properly gassed up
> Hoodie to mask up, sh*t, for that fast buck,
> she be layin in the bushes to light that *ss up
> Number four: know you heard this before
> Never get high, on your own supply
> Number five: never sell no crack where you rest at
> I don't care if they want a ounce, tell 'em bounce
> Number six: that god damn credit, dead it
> You think a crackhead payin' you back, sh*t forget it
> Seven: this rule is so underrated
> Keep your family and business completely separated

> Money and blood don't mix like two d*cks and no
> b**ch
> Find yourself in serious sh*t.[95]

In contrast, the good life according to both the NOI and NGE is actualized once the goal of gaining "knowledge of self" through culture awareness and religious adherence is achieved. While HC acknowledges these two avenues, materialism is the predominant vision of the good life expressed in HC. This is not to say that religious advocacy is not also prevalent. The case can be made, however, that one aspect of rap music that stresses gaining material wealth at any cost is more widespread than those that profess the tenets of the NOI or NGE. The media adds to the crisis. Black media such as radio and Black Entertainment Television (BET), and non-black media such as MTV pander to white audiences. These media deem mindless, pointless songs and apolitical artists as acceptable. Their product is devoid of any redeeming social or political value. Songs that express didactic nihilism ironically are more *acceptable* to radio, video shows and record stores than those categorized as nationalistic or religious. In monetary terms, *acceptable* means commercially viable.

There is tension within HC regarding the ideals and the best method of achieving them. Rallying around the slogan "keep it real,"[96] One school of artists consciously opposes the overt commercialism reflected in materialism and didactic nihilism. They insist that the good life can still be achieved through an understanding of self, culture, cooperative economics and enlightened politics. Underground group, Black Star, makes the point. Talib Kweli, a member of the group, observes that,

> we're played against each other like puppets,
> swearin you got pull when the only pull you got is
> the wool over your eyes
> Gettin knowledge in jail like a blessing in disguise
> Look in the skies for God,
> what you see besides the smog is broken dreams
> flying away on the wings of the obscene
> Thoughts that people put in the air
> Places where you could get murdered over a glare
> But everything is fair

> It's a paradox we call reality
> So keepin' it real will make you casualty of abnormal
>   normality.[97]

Elsewhere he states:

> You can bet, they tryin' to lock you down like Attica,
> The African diaspora represents strength in numbers,
> A giant can't slumber forever;
> Why you gotta get that cheddar whatever;
> I heard you twice the first time money, get it together;
> You must be history, you repeatin' yourself out of
>   the pages;
> You keepin' yourself, depleting your spiritual wealth;
> That quick cash'll get your ass quick fast in houses of
>   detention;
> Inner-city concentration camps where no one pays
>   attention;
> Or mentions the ascension of death, til nothing's
>   left...[98]

The artist known as Common, a veteran of the "keep it real" philosophy, relays a similar message. He admits:

> I'd be lying if I said I didn't want millions
> More than money saved, I wanna save children
> Dealing with alcoholism and Afrocentricity[99]

While artists who indulge in materialism and didactic nihilism enjoy success in the commercial world of HC, they are chastised by some of their peers and HC aficionados. Unfortunately, the medium through which such dissenting expressions are broadcast remain inadequate. The list of artists who convey these ideals are extensive and seem to be gaining momentum.

Agencies, the NOI, NGE and HC

A political philosophy for the most part arises as a challenge to an existing order, provides a vision of a different and more satisfying future, at least to its proponents, and stipulates agencies through which the desired future may be achieved. Thus, the stipulation of agencies is an essential element of a political philosophy.[100] This section ascertains what agencies are associated with the ideals in the political philosophy of both organizations and the extent to which these agencies are reflected in the message conveyed by HC.

The first agency through which the NOI's mission of self-reliance, economic independence and Black Nationalism manifests was business enterprise. Through business enterprises that produce and sell lecture tapes, newspapers, books, videos, and pamphlets, the NOI worldview is disseminated.

Emphasis has been placed on economic self-sufficiency through agriculture production. The purchase of lands from the federal government, the acquisition of heavy machinery and recruitment of fellow Muslims worldwide with expertise in agriculture reflects the economic vision of the NOI. In Los Angeles the establishment of *Your Farmers Market Inc.*, a community market, has been successful. Consumers pay a standard fee, which is below average market value for the goods, and receive a pre-packaged supply of groceries.[101] Other programs such as the *Three Year Economic Program*, which stress saving and investments, are also part of the overall program of economic self-sufficiency.[102] Another agency is the newly formed political wing in the national organization which I identify as the NOI's Political Action Committee (NOIPAC). The purpose of the NOIPAC is to run candidates for elected office from all levels in all states.[103] A second focus is to monitor the agenda and voting record of candidates elected by the black vote. In addition, the mission of a plan of action titled *Agenda 2000* is to challenge America's two-party system. The intent is to demand accountability from both parties and possibly construct a third party. Lack of accountability from the two major parties would lead to a forfeit of the black vote. As one representative of the NOI states, "We believe with this third force that we'll be able to negotiate a much better relationship with both parties. This is a mature position for black people to take and we believe there is a tremendous amount of support for this kind of concept in our community."[104] The establishment of a network of Islamic school named Sister Clara Muhammad school, in honor of the wife of Elijah Muhammad, represents another agency through which the NOI seeks to accomplish its goals. Several of these schools are no longer the sole property of the NOI and now serve the diverse Muslim population.[105] Nonetheless, schools such as the University of Islam were prototypes and predate the present boom in Islamic schools across America. The purpose of these early prototypes of Islamic schools developed by the NOI was to teach the tenets of the NOI as well as the Holy Koran.

While HC has generally affiliated itself with all of the agencies of the NOI, alignment with their agencies is not apparent. It had however, aligned itself with the programs, mission and strategy that emerge from these agencies. For example, concerned artists have on countless occasions used its mosques, ministers and reputation to mediate disputes and to sponsor conferences and fund raisers for various political and social concerns.[106] Even artists who are not official members espouse and declare the political philosophy. For example, the artist Mos Def, affectionately called Chairman Mao (Tse-tung) within Hip Hop circles, frequently describes the condition of Africans in America by using the vernacular of the NOI or evocative references to its leadership.[107]

Agencies of the NGE identified as instruments prescribed by the political philosophy for achieving the good life were developed by Clarence 13X as early as 1967. With reluctant help from the Urban League and Mayor Lindsay's office in New York, Clarence13X established the first street front academy. Since then many academies have been established, most within the tri-state area. Use of the city facilities is often combined with "home schools" to establish learning centers. The most visible is the street academy named *Allah School in Mecca*.

Similar to NOI, agencies through which ideals of the NGE are pursued include economic enterprises. Businesses that specialize in optometry, security, photography, marketing, books, videos and a host of other services reflect the ideal of economic self sufficiency. In 2000, a five-year economic plan to build a seven-story building at the original location of the first academy to serve as NGE headquarters was underway. Other agencies include newspapers and newsletters that move in and out of circulation. They consist of *The Word*, *Builders Always Build*, *The Son of Man*, *The Foundation* and *God on Point*. The newspapers and pamphlets keep members and advocates aware of their accomplishments, community events, local, state, and national politics, actualized goals and challenges facing the organization. These papers are inundated with the lessons and slogans such as "The Black Man is God," "Supreme Mathematics," "Show and Prove" and a range of others. The circulation of the majority of these reached its zenith in the late 1970s and early 1980s. By 2000, the only paper among those listed, which was still in circulation, was *The Word.* New newsletters and online desktop publications have replaced the bi- monthly and monthly periodicals of the NGE.[108] Collectively, these institutions represent the appropriate structures and mechanisms through which the good life could be achieved.

Advocacy of the agencies of NGE and NOI are reflected in HC. Artists express their endorsement of NGE and NOI agencies by attempting to develop similar strategies. For instance, many artists who are independently attempting to produce and distribute their art reflect economic self-independence, throughout HC. The Poor Righteous Teachers (PRT),[109] members of the NGE, typifies the strategy of economic independence. A website allows listeners to hear and purchase their CD major record companies. Others groups such as

G. O. D. from South Bend, Indiana, Solar Panel, a group of independent artists from several different cities, have accomplish similar goals. In fact, many artists are producing records on "white labels." The term is used to denote independently produced and distributed songs. The record physically has a white label, which is a symbol of self production.[110] Other attempts to be economically self sufficient are visible. Several artists, who have gained financial success in HC, have branched off into other endeavors. Queen Latifah, lyricist and producer of several award winning albums, uses her notoriety to produce a talk show, owns her own production company and is a spokesperson for several causes affecting women's lives. Other examples of attempted self-reliance consisting of distribution, marketing, and retail, satiate HC–especially underground HC.

In the political arena, HC has partly adhered to the NOI's strategy of inclusion. Such advocacy is reflected in voter registration drives. Within HC several political action committees, similar to those developed by the NOI, have been established.

For instance, the Hip Hop Coalition for Political Power, an advocacy group, organized and registered nearly 70, 000 people of color between the ages of 18 and 24 as voters.[111] Rappers Educating All Curricula through Hip Hop (REACH), according to its co-founder activist Donna Frisby, attempt to recruit rappers to speak to children and "break down legislative and political concerns for the next generation of young leaders."[112] More notably, artists frequently produce compilation albums to bring awareness to particular political concerns. A few examples are listed below in Table 1.

Table 1: Compilation Albums

SONG TITLE	CAUSE
"Ndodemmnyama"	Hip Hop artist against Apartheid
"We're all in the Same Gang"	Hip Hop artist speaking out against violence
"Mumia 911"	Free Mumia Movement
"Where Ya At"	In support of the Million Man March
"Close the Crackhouse"	Bring attention to the crack epidemic
"No More Prisons"	Promote awareness of the Prison Industrial Complex
"Hip Hop for Respect"	Express outrage at police brutality
"Evolution"	Celebrating black history (month)

These are but a few examples of HC's advocacy of the principles of NGE and NOI agencies.

Ideology, NOI, NGE, and HC

The accepted definition of what constitutes an ideology includes a set of justifying beliefs in terms of which certain institutions and practices are justified and others attacked, and phrases and slogans used in making demands, offering criticism, and exhorting and mobilizing supporters.[113] This section identifies the ideologies of the NOI and NGE that emanate from their theology. In addition, this section identifies whether HC adheres to the ideology of both organizations. Taken together with the other constituent elements, the existence of ideology(ies) within HC would qualify it as a viable political instrument. Thefoundation of an ideology for both NOI and NGE is located in mythology. Such a mythology justifies the divinity of the "Blackman" and the satanic qualities of the Europeans. According to this mythos, the "Blackman" is divine; the white man is a grafted genetic creation of the original who uses "tricknology" or false knowledge dominated the Asiatic "Blackman." The grafted white man in the midst of the righteous, created wars among all the righteous black people. The king banished them to Europe where they remained for a time, only to escape and cause chaos throughout the world in other foreign lands. Even Musa (Moses) could not help them. According to doctrine their time of rule has expired and it is now time for the "Blackman" to rule again.[114] Whether these events occurred as stated is not a central concern. The point is that this mythology represents the root from which evolved a set of self justifying beliefs responsible for shaping the worldview of the NOI.

Consequently, these self-justifying beliefs of the NOI deeply influence HC. They attempt to demonstrate that the historical enemy of black people (Europeans), remain their contemporary enemy, the rightful place of black is at the head of the human family (since black genetics are dominant), the NOI program has the solution to the problems that confront Americans, the duty of the Muslim in America is to civilize the uncivilized and, a utopia can be established through nation building and separatism. Since the NGE is a progeny of the NOI, a similar set of self-justifying beliefs is apparent in the development of its ideology. The set of justifying beliefs of the NGE identified by Aminah Beverly McCloud includes, among other ideas, the belief that black people are the parents of civilization, the original people of Earth. The NGE believes that the science of divine math is the key to understanding man's relationship to the universe. Education should be fashioned to make blacks self-sufficient. Children are the link to the future and they must be nurtured, respected, protected and educated. Thus, the responsibility of each is to teach one according to his or her knowledge. Consequently, the black family is strengthened, which is an essential for nation building.[115]

The NGE dogma is deeply symbolic and believes that mathematic is a universal language. The numbers zero through nine and the twenty-six letters developed by Father Allah create a unique language through which the nation communicates. All members select names that represent positive attributes, which are usually taken from the lessons. For instance, I have spoken with members with names such as Supreme, Divine, Knowledge, Understanding and Wise. In addition, all adopt the name *Allah*. These tenets represent the NGE's theoretic and theologic foundation, which is central to their political philosophy and the development of this compelling worldview. HC adheres to the ideology of both NGE and NOI. HC's earliest history reveals its endorsement.

Subsequent to the initial stage of HC's development where MCs (lyricists) played the dozens, lyrical content became more politicized. Several sources assert that the first politicized rap lyrics come from an artist named Daryl Aamaa Nubyahn, pronounced *Daryl I'm a Nubian*. According to McCloud,

> The toughest talk, though came from Brother D with his *How We Gonna make the Black Nation Rise*, . . . Brother D, a young math teacher named Daryl Aamaa Nubyahn, recorded a hip hop tune to reflect the philosophy of a political and cultural organization called National Black Science.[116]

The initial politicized ideology of HC as a product of religious dogma presented by Brother D is acknowledged. Other earlier manifestations of politicized HC that developed from within the religious - political ideology of the NOI were products of the DJ. Afrika Bambaataa and several other DJs would play long instrumentals[117] that were overlaid with speeches by Malcolm X and other ministers of the Nation of Islam. David Toop suggests that speeches by Martin Luther King were also included. Of the several "old school"[118] participants in HC that I had the opportunity to interview, none have indicated hearing Martin Luther King's speeches but they remember clearly the speeches of Malcolm X while he was a member of the NOI. In 1983, one record label recorded a Malcolm X speech with an instrumental Hip Hop track in the background. The title was "No Sellout" and marked the earliest use of a politicized worldview of the NOI within HC. As Hip Hop culture gained a national audience via recording contracts, MTV and market sales, this method of politicizing black youth found its way into the mainstream culture. Public Enemy was among the first to include samples speeches of Nation of Islam ministers on their albums. Minister Louis Farrakhan's voice in particular is heard on several of Public Enemy's albums. Furthermore, his words articulate the religious ideology that is usually associated with politicized HC. Many artists sample the voices of the NOI representatives who articulate ideologies deem to be controversial or verbally confrontational. For example one album opens with the following words of Louis Farrakhan:

> . . . we don't want nothing but justice,
> thanks to the rappers who have taken the word,
> now the babies are rapping to wisdom
> now you'll never get rid of Farrakhan,
> you'll never get rid of Muhammad
> I am warning you in the name of God Allah, change
>   or die
> the Blackman must have justice.[119]

Between the verses on Public Enemy's *It takes a Nation to Hold Us Back!* Louis Farrakhan's voice is habitually sampled. For instance, he scolds black radio for controlling the minds of blacks with unethical music by lamenting, "you in black radio, how long do you think that we're gonna let you get away with [that]?"[120] Public Enemy went as far as organizing its membership similar to the NOI. A group of black men adorned with military attire and executing military maneuvers called the S1W's (Security of the First World), would accompany the group on stage. The striking resemblance to the NOI's symbolic military wing, the Fruits of Islam, was beyond coincidence. Some members of the group were members of the NOI that obviously represent adherence to its ideology. The use of titles such as "Minister of Information," a Black Panther Party reference, added to the public perception of Public Enemy as revolutionary. Slogans such as "Fight the Power" and "Fear of a Black Planet" continue to echo the ideology of the NOI. Similarly, the songs and lyrics of the group also reflect NOI ideology. For example in a song titled "Fight the Power" the chorus repeats,

> Excuse us for the news
> You might not be amused
> But did you know white comes from Black
> No need to be confused.[121]

Another self-justifying belief of the NOI involves the failure of black leadership. The NOI frequently criticizes mainstream black leadership. The dissatisfaction with black leadership pervades HC also. Many of the artists who echo such sentiments are directly affiliated with the NOI. Artists such as Paris, Kam, Ice T, Da Lynch Mob and, Ice Cube[122] all present critiques of black leadership which seem to be identical to NOI criticisms.

HC's endorsement of NGE ideology is not as obvious and perceptible as the NOI's ideology. Within HC, the language of politics is frequently coded in phrases and verses exclusive to the vernacular of the NGE. This often leads those who are not familiar with the vernacular to believe that a political philosophy is non-existent. Hip Hop artists often cite these lessons in many of their songs in coded symbolic language. Code language has historical roots. Its tradition can be traced back to African slave songs, spirituals, work songs, and story telling. The following examples confirm the point regarding coded language. Method Man, one of HC's most noted artists and an affiliate of the NGE and *Wu- Tang Clan*[123] provides the general sentiment. He laments,

> I fear for the 85 that don't gotta clue
> how could he know what the f**k he never knew
> God cipher divine come to show and come to prove
> a mystery god that's the work of Yakub
> the Holy Ghost got you scared to death kid. . .
> boo!![124]

As described earlier, the "85" represents the uneducated masses. The verse, "god cipher divine come to show and come to prove," simply means that the existence of God is within man and can be empirically supported. These coded phrases developed by NGE saturate the verbal expressions within HC. More importantly the recitations of such political ideologies represent the nucleus of politicized HC.

The critically acclaimed artist, Erykah Badu, is also influenced by the NGE doctrine. Her first single titled "On & On" was number one on several Top 40 pop charts and number two on the Billboard charts for several weeks. Badu's success on R&B radio and her critical appeal make her a household name throughout American pop culture. A closer investigation of the lyrics to the song of this "soulful songstress," as she is descibed by pop culture reveals several references to NGE cosmology. With a raspy Billie Holiday voice, she sings,

> Peace and blessins' manifest with every lesson learned
> If your knowledge were your wealth, then it would
> be well earned
> If we were made in His image then call us by our
> names
> Most intellects do not believe in God but they fear us
> just the same.[125]

Ethic, NOI, NGE and HC

The ethical content of a political philosophy involves normative principles used to judge people and their beliefs, practices and institution that they create and employ.[126] This section identifies an ethic of the NOI and NGE and describes the extent to which it is reflected in HC.

The NOI's ethic is overwhelmingly rooted in its theology. Both the Koran (Qu'ran) and the Bible are used to justify chastisement of its adversaries and support for the NOI's mission. For instance, Matthew 24:27, which reads, "For as the lightning cometh out of the east, and shineth even unto the west, so shall the coming of the son of man be," is often cited by NOI as evidence of the divinity of the "Blackman" in North America.

The principle of building knowledge of self through the adaptation of the black ecumenical liberating philosophy is strikingly similar in NOI and NGE doctrine as well as HC. The Poor Righteous Teachers (PRT), use Christian scripture in a similar method as the NOI and NGE to support their particular worldview.[127] One song suggests,

> politricks and ten percenters who know the truth but

> hold it back from the youth. There's proof that Jesus
>   Christ was
> a so-called spook.
> Revelations Chapter 1:13 and 16 wool hair bronze
>   skin
> Jesus was blacker than me.
> I'll prove and I claim that the truth has been changed;
> For the lies and the white supremacy to remain.
> That chain on your brain makes it hard to maintain.[128]

Nihilism and materialism pose the largest threat to HC's development of useful strategies. As a consequence, HC's harsh critique of undesirable behavior results in an ethic rooted in repudiation and negation. Thus a preponderance of artists emphasize that the good life cannot be achieved without high moral standards. The challenge for African youth in low-income environments to remain dedicated to NOI and NGE's principles is captured by one self-described urban hustler turned Hip Hop artist who remarks:

> We were beginners in the hood as five percenters
> But somethin' must of got in us cause all of us turned
>   to sinners
> Now some, restin in peace and some are sittin in San
>   Quentin
> Others such as myself are tryin to carry on tradition.[129]

Principles such as self-respect, righteousness, seeking knowledge and wisdom and good health constitute the fullness of the ethic for both NGE and NOI and are found throughout HC. Such principles are primarily coded in symbolic language. Self respect, for example, is often articulated utilizing self re identification tools such as the idealized "I." The historical relevance of the idealized "I," is best characterized by Nelson George who suggests,

> the renaming trend is an extension of a long process
> by which African -Americans have created new "I's"
> that speak to how they see themselves or wish to be
> seen. The blues, the roots of most American music
> and the essential idiomatic African-American expres-
> sion, is studded with the new "I's". Muddy Waters
> (once McKinly Morganfield), Bo Diddly (once

Eugene McDaniels), Howlin' Wolf (once Chester Burnett)–all created gutsy new identities that spoke to a grand sense of self.

In addition:

> The first word in Ellison's *Invisible Man* is "I." In some of the most important African-American male narratives of this dying century–Richard Wright's *Black Boy*, Claude Brown's *Manchild in the Promised Land*, James Baldwin's *The Fire Next Time*, Nathan McCall's *Makes Me Wanna Holler*, and the entire canon of rap–a powerful autobiographical impulse demands the exploration of the "I" of me.

Both NOI and NGE view this "autobiographical impulse" or name change as a symbol of self respect based on a new worldview rooted in one's knowledge of self. According to the accepted doctrine of both organizations, the lost tribe of Shabazz (Blacks) in the wilderness of North America must rid themselves of their European slave master's name for it denotes ownership and a lack of "knowledge of self." Many youth inside and outside of HC have renamed themselves using Arabic, Swahili other African languages, and acronyms that reflect positive attributes of self. Countless artists adhere to this act of self-respect. However, the function of this autobiographical impulse should not be overstated. There is an adverse trend in HC that is an extension of the materialism and didactic nihilism described previously. Several artists have re-identified themselves to reflect their advocacy of didactic nihilism. Names such as *Black Menace, C-Murder, Niggaz with Attitude (NWA), Ghetto Mafia, Illegal, Homicide, The Murderers, Pimp Daddy* and many others undermine the intent of self re identification by assigning themselves with labels that merely support the traditional stereotypes of Black youth and HC. It could be argued that if positive re-identification is an act of self-love, negative re identification has the adverse effect; it is an act of self-contempt. HC's attempt to counter such negative portrayal by focusing on self is a penumbra of its ethic. Lauren Hill best articulates this point. She declares,

My world it moves so fast today

The past it seems so far away
And life squeezes so tight that I can't breathe
And every time I try to be,
what someone else has thought of me
So caught up, I wasn't able to achieve
But deep in my heart, the answer it was in me
And I made up my mind to define my own destiny
I look at my environment
And wonder where the fire went
What happened to everything we used to be?
I hear so many cry for help
Searching outside of themselves
Now I know his strength is within me
And deep in my heart, the answer it was in me
And I made up my mind to define my own destiny
And deep in my heart, the answer it was in me
And I made up my mind to define my own destiny.

Hill's album title pays homage to Carter G. Woodson's text *The Mis-Education of the Negro*. These issues considered self re-identification in HC is rooted in the language, doctrine and ultimately the ethic of the NOI and the NGE.

The notion of righteous is another principle found in the NOI and NGE's ethic. According to both, only the righteous will experience freedom, justice and equality. Righteousness, according to the doctrine of both groups, is gained by adhering to the laws and instructions of Allah.[130] Righteousness in HC has fewer stringent requirements and bears a somewhat different definition. One would be considered righteous according to HC if she demonstrates a sense of culture and history, a sense of politics, (race, class and gender included), and religious advocacy. For example, the group Dead Prez is considered righteous artists primarily because their art addresses America's problems with black solutions. Discussions of police corruption, exploitative capitalism, spirituality, African nationalism, healthy living, self-love, and many other pertinent issues that affect black people are the central focus of their lyrics. Dead Prez's ethic is developed from a black nationalist philosophy of Marcus Garvey, Malcolm X and Elijah Muhammad. Thus the connection to the ethic of NGE and NOI, while not obvious is nonetheless present. Songs such as "I'm an African" in which the words such as, "I'm an African, never was an African-American, blacker than black, I take it back to my origin…" and "No, I wasn't born in Ghana, but Africa is my momma, and I did not end up here from bad karma…"[131] represent a valuable example of how righteousness is defined and articulated in HC. However, that righteousness in HC does not necessarily indicate adherence to NGE and NOI doctrine. For example, the group Goodie Mob, considered to be righteous members of the Hip Hop community, includes Christian theology as a central component of their ethic and consequent political philosophy. This view is reflected in the following verse.

> Lord it's so hard, living this life
> A constant struggle each and every day
> Some wonder why I'd rather die
> Than to continue living this way
> Many are blind and cannot find the truth
> Cause no one seems to really know
> But I won't accept that this is how it's gon' be
> Devil you gotta let me and my people go
> Cause I wanna be free, completely free
> Lord won't you please come and save me
> I wanna be free, totally free I'm not gon' let this
>   world worry me.[132]

These lyrics read more like a spiritual than the creation of Hip Hop lyricists. Their ability to infuse a spiritual and political philosophy in their music provides an ethic for HC. That said, righteousness as articulated in HC, overwhelmingly had its roots in the doctrine of NOI and NGE. With few exceptions including the group discussed above, the majority of Hip Hop artists described as "righteous" are members or affiliates of NGE or NOI.

Other aspects of an ethic supported by the NOI and the NGE relate to good health. The text, *How to Eat and Live* written by Elijah Muhammad, is the bible of good health for both organizations. Instruction on proper diet, physical and mental health and general instructions to support a healthy lifestyle are also found in the lessons of the NGE called "The 120" (120 degrees of lessons). The prohibition to partake in eating swine is perhaps the most repeated regulation. HC often scolds parents for feeding their children pork, warns of dangerous chemical additives in foods and supports a healthy lifestyle including vegetarianism. Artists such as KRS-ONE, not only advocate an end to pork consumption, but all meat. He remarks,

> Any drug is addictive by any name
> Even drugs in meat, they are the same
> The FDA has America strung out
> On drugs in beef no doubt
> So if you think that what I say is a bunch of crock
> Tell yourself you're gonna try and stop
> Eatin' meat and you'll see you can't compete
> It's the number one drug on the street
> Not crack, cause that was made for just Black
> But brown beef, for all American teeth
> Life brings life and death brings death
> Keep on eatin' the dead and what's left?
> Absolute disease and negative
> Read the book 'How to Eat to Live' By Elijah
>   Muhammad,
> it's a brown paperback
> For anybody, either white or black
> See how many cows must be pumped up fatter
> How many rats gotta fall in the batter
> How many chickens that eat sh*t you eat
> How much high blood pressure you get from pig
>   feet
> See you'll consume, the FDA could care less
> They'll sell you donkey meat and say it's FRESH![133]

The ethic of the NGE and NOI is visible in HC. Nonetheless, total commitment to these principles remains a challenge. The triumph of truth over falsehoods, self-respect over self-contempt, and righteousness over didactic nihilism are goals to be achieved. As HC becomes more diverse, a contemporaneous variety of Hip Hop music has emerged. While theologically divergent from the NOI or NGE, this new variety attempts to contribute a similar ethic to HC. This new form is identified as Christian Hip Hop.

Chapter IV
GOD IS HIP HOP

Christian Hip Hop: an Oxymoron?

During the late 1990s, there has been a move in the African religious community to reclaim youth as members as well as active participants in the black churches. Some churches and clergy have supported this effort through talents searches, concerts and spoken word contests. Overall, the church has reluctantly embraced Hip Hop and there is furious debate between those who see HC as a vehicle to glorify God and reach youth and those traditionalists who believe that the value of the church is compromised if it attempts to use what is generally viewed as evil and sinful music to spread its message. Some in the Hip Hop community believe that true Hip Hop must reject Christianity because it camouflages black reality with religious abstractions. Many in the Christian community believe that true Christianity must reject HC because it contradicts all the tenets of Christianity. Nonetheless, a new music form termed Christian Hip Hop attempts to mediate.[134]

Independent Christian artists are producing music that celebrates "Jesus as Lord." Some reflect the need for a new liberation strategy, but the majority simply repeats the bible verses and the traditional theology partly responsible for the flight and disillusionment of youth in the first place. MC Hammer was among the first to present Christian rap. His song titled "Pray" enjoyed some commercial success. According to one writer on the subject, Christian Hip Hop has recently offered a more aggressive message. While the precursors of Christian Hip Hop had almost nothing to say about the life and death problems and issues considered "worldly" by the old-style gospel, "Christian hip-hop may turn out to be the single prophetically pragmatic voice in a new postmodern Christianity, a voice uninhibited by powers that be diplomacy."[135]

Artists attempting to bridge the gap between Hip Hop and Christianity include the following:

PID (Preachers in Disguise)	ETW (End of Time Warriors)
SFCC (Soldiers for Christ)	DC Talk
Fresh Fish	Witness
Gospel Gangstaz	Two Edge
GRITS	Know Da Verbs

Many new Christian Hip Hop artists are presenting a more radical Christian message. The Africanity of Jesus, the corruption of messages and messengers, moral failure and the general failure of black theology are issues articulated inside this new music form. There are some skeptics who view the present popularity of Christian Hip Hop as having less to do with truth, justice and morality and more to do with market mechanisms. This problem is also pervasive with HC. One critic captures the controversy, as she remarks, "Bible toting teens account for the 32 percent growth rate gospel music has enjoyed over the past five years. Many record labels have cashed in on the popularity of gospel music and its appeal to a generation with an impressive amount of disposable income." [136]

According to SoundScan, 19,830,000 units were sold between January 1 and July 2001; an increase of 2.2 million units. The same source reports that "urban-gospel departments" represents 25% of all Christian sales. Radio stations in search of cash cows have been steadily converting program format to appeal to Christian audiences. Market research has indicated that consumers are tired of the didactic nihilism and overt sexism that is pervasive within commercial mainstream Hip Hop. Ironically, those very institutions responsible for promoting and encouraging these one dimensional depictions of black life also profit from the sale of God music with a Hip Hop orientation. Consequently marketers and other purveyors of poison profit from spreading both the poison and the antidote.

Gospel music has long been infused in secular culture. As black music dictates, the spiritual realm has led to the secular, and the secular to the popular-spiritual. The popular-spiritual may seem oxymoronic to some and some of the artists may simply be classed as moronic. I will address that point later. By popular-spiritual we mean those products that reflect large sales. Examples of these would be the Winans, Mary Mary, Yolanda Adams, Donnie McClurkin, and Kirk Franklin. Their antecedents include Aretha Franklin, Cee Cee Winans and Shirley Caesar, who have revolutionized the industry of gospel music and thus opened the door for Hip Hop Gospel to thrive. Their approval or disapproval of the new variety of gospel music will not be debated here but will be discussed shortly in this chapter. Kirk Franklin and a host of others have also contributed greatly to the popularity and growth. As gospel artists begin to increase Christian Hip Hop's visibility through crossover and guess appearances on Christian Hip Hop albums, more noted Hip Hop lyricists have added to legitimizing Christian Hip Hop.

KRS One, affectionately and respectfully called "the teacher" and "philosopher" of rap, is perhaps the most noted. Chris has been a spiritual voice in Hip Hop for almost twenty years. He has addressed the moral degradation of humanity in similar terms to that of traditional Christian theology. These include devotion to God, counteracting moral decay of humanity and spiritual cleansing, all of which have reflected a clear set of instruction on how to live a righteous life. What is odd at times is that previously he has frequently rebuked what he has called "so called Christians." This idea is not original. It is the song that some atheists and non-atheists sing to defend the position that Christianity is full of irreversible contradiction. Afrocentrists use(d) it to signify and justify the Kemetic origin of Christianity: books such as *Echoes of the Old Darkland, Pagan Origin of the Christ Myth, Christianity Before Christ, Rebirth of Christianity, Ages of Gold and Silver, YURUGU, The Councils of Nicea, Man, God, and Civilization, African Origins of Civilization* and other texts authored by Gerald Massey, John G. Jackson, Martin Bernal, Anthony Browder, Dr.Ben Jochannan. While the credibility of these texts has been heavily debated, the most politicized elements within Hip Hop are exposed to them and make reference to them periodically within their lyrics. KRS does not make specific mention of these books or authors but the content of his songs clearly indicates some exposure. For example, while discussing the connectedness of religion, astrology and astronomy he repeats a position that most of the writers listed above included in their writing:

> This age is coming to an end
> Not the world, but the age is ending
> Ending, listen to the astrological message I'm sending
> I'm sending, tell 'em
> Truth is truth, whether or not you like me
> We are now living in the age of Pisces
> When Pisces is over, at the year two thousand
> When the Sun of God, changes his house and
> Enters the Age of Aquarius
> The Sun of God as man is hilarious (okay)
> When you think of Jesus, think of the Sun
> The flaming Sun, that's where they stole this concept
>   from
> Stop believing and read your bible logically
> The New Testament is really old astrology
> Jesus is the son of God no lie
> But they might be talking about the Sun up in the sky
> The Sun, that hangs on the cross of the zodiac
> The zodiac with twelve signs to be exact
> Each sign is a house, and you should keep in mind
> Each house equals, a period of time
> The time, two thousand years and that's a fact
> It's called an age or a house in the zodiac
> The twelve disciples, are twelve months of reason
> The four gospels signify the four seasons
> When Jesus fed the multitude with two fishes
> It signified the Age of Pisces, not fish or dishes
> If you read the bible astrologically it's clearer (no
>   doubt)
> The next age will be the age of the water-bearer

It's called the Age of Aquarius (word)
When logic and truth will take care of us
So in this age, of spiritual dignity
You'll see a rise in femininity
And creativity, meshed with masculinity
You got to get with me; this is your true her-story[137]

Several other songs on his previous albums indicate the similar intolerance of those who misinterpret scripture. Recently, however, his brass freestyle condemnation has mellowed and in fact he has incorporated Christianity in one album title *Spiritual Minded*. He clearly saw the need to incorporate Hip Hop and Christianity. He understood that he was the catalyst to do so and that an affiliation with Christian Hip Hop compliments his mission. In addition, he would reach a wider audience other the Hip Hop purists that were loyal to his position as Hip Hop's holy intellect. Christian Hip Hop needed an authentic voice of Hip Hop to articulate its vision and reach the masses representative of "real" Hip Hop. Thus the relationship has mutual gain. If one of Christianity's goals is to proselytize, Christian Hip Hop artists need to reach beyond its core audience. Reverend Run of Run DMC is commended for adorning himself with a cross instead of the trademark Adidas shoes. He will be remembered for the former and not the latter.

Many new artists of Christian Hip Hop are ministers, reverends and pastors. This new phenomenon may be directly related to pioneers such as Reverend Run's outward expression of God first, Hip Hop second.

Living Water or Iced Out

The June 2002 issue of *Essence* magazine contained an article that expressed not a new crisis but a devastating crisis involving young black women. *Essence* had been publishing various authors writings and diverse subjects under the heading *The War on Girls*. Joan Morgan, a proclaimed Hip Hop feminist, wrote an interesting article titled, "Sex, Lies, and Videos." Joan's major thesis is that the image of black women is distorted and overly sexualized. Consequently, it is sending the wrong message to young black girls about self-worth and self-esteem. Media such as BET (Black Entertainment Television) broadcasts what she calls "near-pornographic images" to its predominantly young black audience. She adds that these one-dimensional images of black women and black womanhood are tolerated and resistance is lacking. Her solution is to demand (from these institutions that play these videos) accountability or a national boycott of stations as well as advertisers to commence. She remarks, "I bet we would see changes then. We would see, perhaps a space where our girls can enjoy the music they love, without risking their self-esteem and souls in the process."[138]

Other than for the fact that I enjoy reading Joan Morgan's work, I bring up this issue for the following reason. As a result of the surge in Gospel and Christian Hip Hop, a disturbing trend is visible. One might assume that Christian Hip Hop would be a "space where our girls can enjoy the music they love, without risking their self-esteem and soul in the process" as Joan puts it, but this is not necessarily the case. More and more, the same images broadcast within Christian Hip Hop are those usually visible in the secular realm. Minus the nudity, the tight form fitting clothes, and the mannerisms (walk with what Caribbean people call whin' and some male artists intolerable rantings) are not so divergent from the secular Hip Hop it intends to counter. The content in many songs seem a bit problematic as well. Yet, some of those gospel tracks "lifted" or "inspired" by Hip Hop seem to be designed, frankly, to get you to shake your ass. Culture critic Michael Eric Dyson captures the paradox. Though his example is specific to Gospel music, his avowal is applicable to Christian Hip Hop. After giving praise to the Winans for making gospel music more mainstream, Dyson suggests that groups including the Winans highlight the implicit sexuality of gospel music. He suggests that at times the repressed relationship between body and soul reflects a suggestive ambiguity of romantic love and sensuous delight camouflaged as deep spiritual yearning for fulfillment. He states:

> In "Depend On You" the Winans sing, "I Never
> Thought That I Could Ever Need Someone/The Way
> That I Have Come To Need You/Never Dreamed I'd

Love Someone/The Way I've Fallen In Love With You."[139]

"Such lyrics," Dyson continues, "are exactly the problem, according to the traditionalists. Whereas traditional gospel music talks about the love of God, contemporary gospel music wants to make love to God." [140] While Dyson's view may be extreme, it highlights a real dilemma. Proponents of Christian Hip Hop believe that it has been a good Christian mission to find sheep that are astray and use their worldview to contextualize, proselytize, and develop a ministry. They believe that if Hip Hop influences young people, Christianity must morph into Hip Hop to reach those participants in the culture—a sensible strategy, except that the lines between secular and spiritual are fraught with inconsistencies. For instance, if one would declare himself a "gangsta" for Jesus, would the declaration of the word "gangsta" not evoke its traditional meaning? That is comparable to declaring oneself a killer, extortionist, criminal, and thug for Jesus. Another problem with Christian Hip Hop is the use of rhythm tracks from traditional Hip Hop song where lyrical misogyny, violence, and nihilism is replaced with declaratory scriptures about believing, and upholding the Christian ethic of love, brotherhood and compassion. Any layperson or Hip Hop aficionado would agree that hearing a remixed Christianized version of a song evokes the secular parent that created it. For example, if a secular song that suggests we "get crunk" is replaced by a song that suggests we "get crunk for Jesus," the latter will automatically evoke the former. We assume that is not the intent but that certainly is the outcome.

Certainly, Christian Hip Hop needs to reach the streets, but celebrating street life as an acceptable trade off to reach evangelical goals is an ineffective strategy. Ratified spirituality with Christian Hip Hop still evokes the traditional secular paradigm and operates within it. The apparent confusion as to when and where the secular becomes the spiritual and the spiritual becomes the secular, remains an important future debate.

Chapter V
HC AND THE POLITICAL ECONOMY OF BLACK RADIO

The preceding chapters determined that there is a discernible political philosophy imbedded in Hip Hop. Works reflecting that philosophy are referred to as politicized Hip Hop. Even though politicized Hip Hop is not the dominant tendency within the genre, it commands the allegiance of a significant number of artists and their followers. Whether or not politicized Hip Hop becomes a major force in youth culture, however, will be determined to a great extent by the level of support or endorsement received from radio, particularly black radio. What is the extent to which black radio through its programming and related activities enhance or diminish the cultural impact of politicized Hip Hop? An answer to this question requires an examination of the programming decisions of black radio to determine the extent to which it promotes or fails to promote the works of politicized Hip Hop artists, an explanation of the variables that determine programming decisions of black radio. These include patterns of radio station ownership, market dynamics, government regulations, rating systems, and control(ed) format. Data from which answers will be derived came from case studies or four Atlanta radio stations, two commercial[141] and two none commercial stations.[142]

History of Black Radio

As early as the 1920s, blacks participated in radio programming. Personalities such as Duke Ellington, Cab Calloway, and Paul Robeson were showcased during the 1930s. These exceptions aside, however, black radio originated and evolved within the strictures imposed by American racism. Consequently, early American radio acknowledged the presence of black life but devoted little programming time for Black audiences. For the most part, black people were presented in negative stereotypical terms. Negative images such as mammy, coon, buck, and tom were dominant.

By the 1940s, white radio stations owners, driven by the desire to maximize profits, recognized black listeners as an untapped market and began to introduce formats that catered to black audiences. The first stations to cater to the black audience included WDIA in Memphis,[143] KUDL in Kansas City, WGES in Chicago, WERD in Atlanta and WWRL in New York.[144] Radio stations which traditionally ignored the black audience began to introduce formats including the blues, and rhythm and blues. The introduction of these new formats led to radio stations playing what was called "race music." The predominant "race music," gospel, was responsible for breaking the color barrier.

By the latter decades of the twentieth century with the rise of highly segmented marketing and radio programming, black radio had become a major medium for socialization and communication within the black community. Community leaders expected black radio to promote interests and causes championed by race leaders. At the same time, however, black radio, owned predominantly by whites and a few blacks, had become lucrative businesses by following an essentially apolitical format that sold Black culture as just another commodity. The juxtaposition of the two positions presented a crisis of function.

Black Radio and its Crisis of Function

The crisis of function regarding black radio is partly obscured by the crisis of ownership. That is, emphasis is placed on the lack of black ownership. The premise is that more black ownership automatically translates to valuable services for these communities. The most recent study on black radio ownership echoes these very presumptions. According to a 1997 report published by The National Telecommunications and Information Administration in conjunction with the Minority Telecommunications

Development Program (MTDP),[145] entitled *Black Commercial Broadcast Ownership*, blacks own 168 of the 10,315 commercial AM and FM stations in the United States. Blacks own 68 of 5,591 (1.2%) commercial FM radio stations. The figure for AM stations is 100 of 4,724 or (2.1%). There are 90 black owners of commercial radio stations. Single proprietors own sixty-three stations and the remaining 27 are group owned. Bishop L. E. Willis, President of Willis Broadcasting, owns a total of 21 stations and Cathy Hughes, CEO of Radio One, owns 13 commercial radio stations.[146] These two represent the largest and second largest single minority owner of commercial radio, respectively. The survey notes that blacks own a significantly larger amount of AM stations than FM stations. Though there was an increase of 867 more FM stations in 1997 than the previous year, FM stations owned by African-American remained low and were barely affected by the increase. The lower costs of AM stations partly explain the higher ownership rate by blacks. Because AM radio's sound quality and range is inferior to FM radio, its signal reaches fewer listeners. Competitive advertising dollars are consequently deferred to the FM stations. The lack of investment and/or venture capital has created a quasi-oligopoly. Many FM stations are owned by a few owners. The findings indicate that "media concentration" or ownership of many stations by a few multimedia organizations has and continues to impede minority ownership of radio stations. Such losses result in fewer employment opportunities for minorities and contribute to the lack of diversity in all aspects of broadcast media including programming.[147] The table below (table 2) lists the top ten radio groups. Though Willis Broadcasting and Radio One have market power, if both companies combined, they would fall short of inclusion on the list of top ten of both revenue and ownership.

Table 2. Top Ten Radio Groups
Ranked by Revenue (in millions) [148]

COMPANY	NUMBER OF STATIONS	1997 REVENUE
Cbs	160	$1,529.4
Chancelor Media Corp*	108	996.0
Jacor Communications	204	602.2
Capstar Broadcasting*	299	537.7
Clear Channel Comm	196	452.3
Abc Radio	29	310.4
Cox Radio	59	246.9
Emmis Broadcasting	13	156.7
Heftel Broadcasting	39	155.5
Susquehanna Radio	21	141.4

According to many, *The Telecommunication Act of 1996* exacerbates the problem of minority ownership by reducing single market ownership qualifications. A more detailed explanation of the legislation is provided below.

Black Radio and The Telecommunications Act of 1996

The Telecommunications Act of 1996 (TCA) represents an overhaul of telecommunications law not seen since 1934. Radio has been impacted by the new legislation. The major areas of concern for black radio are ownership and market share. The new legislation allows a single owner to own as many as eight stations in a single market. Prior to the 1996 legislation, media ownership was limited to a *total* of twelve stations. As one reporter noted, "The consolidation of the industry has happened within 12 months as 20 companies now control 30 percent of the radio stations in the country."[149] As mergers continue almost monthly, a few companies controlling hundreds of stations is rapidly becoming the standard not the exception. These companies have less interest in social service and respond mostly to stockholders. In an attempt to be competitive, many black stations operate no different from their market competitors whose bottom line is profit not politic. More specifically, politicized information is rarely conveyed on radio programming that targets Hip Hop listeners who would benefit from such. A closer look at Atlanta radio reveals that even though some programming do in fact incorporate community concerns, these programs are not specifically geared to its younger audience, a point which is corroborated by the case studies below.

Atlanta Black Radio Stations Case Studies

As indicated earlier, the determination of whether Black radio enhanced the impact of politicized Hip Hop, requires the examination of the programming practices and related activities of four Atlanta stations that feature Hip Hop music. Two of them were commercial stations WHTA-FM and WVEE-FM, and two were none commercial, WRFG a non-profit community station and WRAS owned by a local college, Georgia State University. All four stations appeal to African American audiences but only WVEE is black owned. I examined the stations' program content and their community involvement to determine the level of support given to politicized Hip Hop and related social causes.

WRFG: "The Voice of the Atlanta Community"

The station was founded in 1973, initially broadcasting at 10 watts. WRFG (89.3) in 2001 broadcast at one hundred thousand watts twenty-four hours a day, seven days a week. Its primary focus in programming is geared toward African American between the ages of 18 and 55, but the station offers programming geared toward Latino, East Indian, African, Caribbean, Celt and other cultures. Its mission is "to provide a broadcast channel for those traditionally denied access to the electronic media and, to popularize and preserve indigenous forms of cultural expression."[150]

News programs which address community concerns include *Pacifica News, Democracy Now, Labor Forum, Counter Spin* and a host of community related forums.[151] The station operates as an electronic bulletin board announcing events from street fairs to community board meetings. Community involvement of WRFG is unmatched in Atlanta. Such community involvement has relevance for youth. The relevance is found in its support for outreach programs as the Lambda report, and the "Panther Power Hour." The "Panther Power Hour" is a program specifically designed to address the concerns of black youth in crisis. Other temporary programming, such as "Spiritual Pimps" was very popular with youth. This program in particular struck a cord with youth for its unabridged and scathing criticism of black Christian ministers in Atlanta. Its audience was primarily youth. While this program has disappeared from the air, WRFG's daily rotation includes Hip Hop, which at times confronts these very concerns. These programs provide the best attempt at presenting politically relevant material for youth in Atlanta. One show in particular, titled *Beats and Lyrics*, presents the most politicized Hip Hop. The program has two hosts, J Force and IRAS, and they alternate weekly. Beyond the politicized music, guests usually discuss the direction of Hip Hop, community police relations, news and events that affect youth in Atlanta. For the last few years, the show has broadcast twenty-four hours during the Freaknik Weekend.[152] One segment of the show called "*Uncensored for Reasoning*," features songs specifically designed to spark dialogue about concerns of black youth and the Hip Hop community. The host, IRAS, believes that HC has the responsibility to teach and develop political ideologies, not betray the contributions of those that struggled in the past. He suggests that "the music must reflect the mood of black youth even if people are uncomfortable with what is being said."[153] Hip Hop enthusiasts, including artists and the general public, call in and voice their concerns. Lyricists frequently visit the studio to participate in the dialogue. There are no official numbers of exactly how many people listen to the program. The phone rings continuously throughout the evening, which does indicate that the number of listeners is significant. Listeners' opinions are central to the programming. The overwhelming concern of the majority of callers is race. While race is not the only subject discussed, it dominates the exchange. Inter- and intra-racial conflict, race pride, righteousness, and racial self-hatred not only dominate the dialogue but the music as well. Other topics for discussion include class and wealth issues, the state of HC, political events and issues not generally presented in the mainstream media such as homosexuality and HC. The show is never without controversy. In May 2000 the topic, commonly referenced as the case for the "white negro," caused some tension not only in the Hip Hop community but among few of the diverse volunteers at the station. The term "White Negro" was used by Norman Mailer in a 1957 essay by the same name. In the essay he states, "So there was a new breed of adventurers; who drifted out at night looking for action with a black man's code to fit their facts. The hipster has absorbed the existentialist synapses of the Negro, and for all practical purposes could be considered a White Negro."

The term is used to invoke similar description of white participants in Hip Hop. The existence of what many insiders call a Hip Hop civil war is apparent. Racial tensions often surface. Mainstream media programs such as *Nightline*,[154] which reported that Hip hop culture brings cultures together, may not be aware of these currents in HC. White suburbanites purchasing Gangsta rap CDs and attending concerts hardly qualify as cultural exchange. Who is and ought to be the voice of Hip Hop is the major source of tension. Whites who embrace HC in many cases may not be consumers, but they own the means and modes of production to advance HC. For example, most periodicals, labels and distribution chains are owned by whites.[155] Similar to their parents with soul music and grandparents with the blues, many black youth view this as the latest manifestation of exploitation and fascination of the "exotic other," where no effective attempt is made to change the traditional hostility waged by the dominant culture against blacks. Consequently, in the minds of many black youth, such turmoil is emblematic of a macroproblem of race and class privileges that whites enjoy. Ironically the medium used to broadcast counterpoints have recently been inundated with white artists. Many callers and advocates of the radio program are concerned that *art for art sake* will replace *art as propaganda*. Despite some pressure, the program has not strayed from its black nationalist position.

J Force, the other biweekly host, focuses most of his effort on informing the community about issues specific to the Hip Hop industry and uses his program to feature underground HC, much of which contains instructive material. In his words, "programming must reflect the variety of views of young people. In addition those with some knowledge of the issues that confront Blacks need a platform. The commercial stations do not offer such opportunities. It is our duty to make sure that all voices of the Hip Hop spectrum are heard."[156]

The program enjoys a general popularity among Atlanta's underground HC and is rapidly growing. Another effective program from WRAS which delivers politicized elements of HC is called *From the Tape Deck to the Studio*. The program, according to its host, Malik Kalaam, features "one of a kind underground conscious Hip Hop." The program fulfills its mission, but it airs on Thursday nights from 2:00 am to 6:00 am. Access to a wider audience is only possible by using a website which rebroadcasts the programs using stream audio technology. The program's mission *is* community involvement and such involvement has relevance for youth. Finally, several shows are specifically targeted at the youth Hip Hop audience. These factors taken together indicate that WRFG enhances the impact of politicized HC.

WRAS–88.5 (Georgia State University Radio)

1971 marked the first broadcast year of Georgia State University, previously called Georgia State College. Since then the station has grown and provides a platform for all genre of music to be broadcast. Presently the station is student operated. Programming includes heavy metal, blues, gothic, jazz, alternative rock and Hip Hop to name a few. Its signal is supported by one hundred thousand watts.

Community involvement is not a specific mandate of the station. The extent of community involvement is reflected in Public Service Announcements (PSA). According to its bylaws, PSA's must be non-profit and must first be approved by the general manager, program director or PSA staff. These PSAs are aired at minimum twice a day and can be no longer than sixty seconds. Most PSAs are health related, addressing issues such as anti-smoking campaigns, driver safety, cancer prevention and water preservation. While informative to the community at large, the extent of its political effectiveness on youth is minimal for several reasons. First, most black youth listeners (usually the student body) tune into programming specifically geared to their interest; exposure is thereby limited since such announcements are aired a few times daily. Second, these have little politicized agendas and reflect more social than political utility. Even campaigns aimed at convincing youth to vote take no partisan or bipartisan positions. Thus WRAS's community involvement while commendable has minimal political utility specifically for youth and HC at large.

The programming offers a bit more access to politicized material. The programs which offer Hip Hop music at the station are, *The Bomb*, *True School Hip Hop*, *Rhythm and Vibes*, and the *New School Hour*. According to John Bennett, the media advisor for the university, programming is decided by student music directors who choose the music that will be placed in regular rotation.[157] Ultimately, program content is based on the judgment of the DJ and program host. The play list of specialty programming is left to the shows' host. The only guideline is that the students take a course, earn certification for an FCC license, sign a contract not to accept payola and follow FCC regulations regarding obscene speech and hate speech.[158] Generally, all of these programs provide a mélange of Hip Hop music, some of which are politicized. Most, however, reflect the artistic and creative side of HC which is generally not associated with any specific political ideology. The most popular of these shows, *Rhythm and Vibes*, presents the best opportunity for politicized Hip Hop to be heard. One of the alternating hosts, Marcel, suggested that preference is always given to artists with politicized lyrics. While his commitment is reflected in programming, the majority of other hosts offer minimal programming advancing any political agenda as advocated within HC. Ultimately, research indicates that WRAS generally does not enhance the impact of politicized HC, aside from those exceptions listed above; no recognizable consistent political ideology advanced by HC is located in its programming.

Unlike the previous two stations examined, the two commercial stations rely heavily on control formats and industry trade publications. The political economy of commercial stations is profoundly shaped by these elements. Hence, the role and function of these agencies provided below is followed by a case study of both stations.

Control Formats, Industry Trade Publications and Hip Hop

The control format describes a system through which radio programmers use research data from industry trade publications to decide programming. This format evolved from a play list report published in 1958 by Bill Gavin, appropriately called Bill Gavin's Record Report. Consequent reports were adopted by WINS in New York, WHDH in Boston, WITH in Baltimore, WGST in Atlanta and KJOY in California. Since its early history, the report has included market share research, regional demographic research and a host of other research services sold to major radio station clients nationwide. *The Gavin Report*, as it is now called, is one of the most reputable industry trade publications with clients nationwide. Its major function is to report sales patterns of various genres of music by region, time period, date and other demographics such as race, age and gender. Thanks to Gavin and a few other trade publications such as Billboard, Hip Hop has been able to demonstrate its true sales power and market influence over the past decade. Major record companies rely heavily on these reports and establish partnerships with the trade. A similar international media research firm and radio industry trade publication is Arbitron. This corporation consists of "three core businesses: measuring radio audiences in local markets across the United States; surveying the retail, media and product patterns of local market consumers; and providing survey research consulting and methodological services to the cable, telecommunications, direct broadcast satellite, online and new media industries."[159]

Arbitron develops its radio data through sampling. Much like the Nielsen rating for television, it relies on diaries distributed to the public to gain data regarding listening habits. The data collection instrument is a seven-day journal maintained by the listener. Listeners are usually offered a minimal fee to complete the diary and return it to the company. Once this is achieved, Arbitron catalogues the results by income, ethnic group and region. Ultimately, it provides a range of marketing and sales information which informs its clients of the spending behavior, education level, and other data of its listeners. Radio stations, including the two examined below, purchase these profiles. The data determines the rates which marketers will be charged to showcase their products on these radio stations. The aim is to gain the highest ratings through listenership, which will command the high advertising rates. As a result, decisions regarding what will be broadcast have less to do with social commitment and more to do with market forces.

Other research instruments such as SoundScan, which directly reports album sales at point of purchase, have a similar impact on HC. SoundScan is a data collection system which tabulates record sales. Sales are counted by scanning the bar code of a record at the retail counter. Most major retail chains transaction are tracked by the SoundScan system. For Hip Hop this system is both detrimental and beneficial. It is beneficial because it offers a national marketplace for artists who otherwise would not have access. It is detrimental for Hip Hop in that those artists who gain national recognition because of this are usually apolitical and in many cases reinforce stereotypical ideas about African-Americans. Black radio is more likely to select these artists for air play. For example *No Limit Records*, perhaps the most successful label in the past few years has benefited tremendously from this system.[160] These artists including the CEO, produce no socially redeeming music.[161]

The SoundScan system provided data that reflected the sale potential of their music. Thus, major distribution deals were established making *No Limit Records* one of the most profitable rap institutions. The chart below confirms the sales power of *No Limit Records*.

Table 3. NLR Sales Estimates
(in thousands)[162]

Label	1996	1997	1998	1999	Total
No Limit	1019	6032	11150	4135	22336

Record executives in search of guaranteed profit sign similar acts that reflect didactic nihilism. Consequently, one-dimensional images of black life as reflected through commercial rap music are not only supported but actively perpetuated through record deals offered to artists who advance stereotypes of blacks for the escapist entertainment of America. More important, America is not exposed to these artists who describe the complexities of black life in America and counter the distortions.

Technology has produced another tracking system that reportedly is a more efficient way of tracking radio listening habits. It is called Mobiltrak. Though limited only to car radio tracking, this system does not use journals but reports exactly what station a listener has tuned into. The system works in the following manner. A device identifies the frequency emitted from cars on the road. The frequency identifies the station. The data is offered to subscribers via the Internet. Unlike the other systems, the data is almost in real time and the sample size is eighty thousand, which is more than twice the size of other reporting agencies. As soon as the signal from the car is identified, it is computed and added to the database. While this system is a bit more efficient, it has some limitations. First, it only targets cars, not homes, work, or retail chains where listening may also occur. Second, it only tracks frequency not amplitude. In other words, FM data is collected but AM data cannot be assessed. Third, counting the same cars more than once is very possible since people travel back and forth. Nonetheless, this system is gaining wide use in many markets and is increasingly replacing the traditional trade publications. Mobiltrak's data during its test run revealed that WHTA (Hot 97.5), one of the two commercial rap stations in Atlanta and focus of this research, has the highest rating.[163]

WHTA (Hot 97.5) "Doing Good in the Hood"

WHTA first aired in 1995. It is owned and operated by Radio One, one of the two most successful minority owners of radio. Since its establishment, the station has carved out a significant market share in Atlanta and competes with its competitor, WVEE, for the urban Hip Hop market. Community outreach and involvement, while not central to the station's economic vision, are nonetheless apparent. A list of community activities sponsored by WHTA is listed below.

WHTA Community Involvement Program
This list includes events from January to June 2000.

Americorps Celebration
GA State Community Service Day
Atlanta Hawks Toy Drive
Eagle Scout Health Fair
Career Fair.Com Live Event
Hosea Williams Feed the Hungry Live Broadcast
Edwin Moses Huggs Run
Dekalb College Voter Registration
Egleston Scottish Rite Gingerbread Contest
Hot 97.5 "Rocks the Vote"
Evander Holyfield Pep Rally
Project Phoenix
Gamma Epsilon Society Cotillion Ball
Hot 97.5 Hair Cuts for the Holidays
Hands on Atlanta Day
AM. Diabetes Walk-A-Thon
Holiday Clothing Drive@ Greenbriar Mall
American Red Cross Tupac Blood Drive
Hot 97.5 Arthritis Foundation's Mini-Grand Prix
Hot Shots Diabetes B-Ball Game
Money Talks Seminar
Hot Shots for Hope Game
Official Atlanta Rock the Vote Station
Love and Understanding Benefit
Read Across Atlanta
Hot 97.5 Mayor's Celebrity Softball Game
Tax Day Preparation@Greenbriar Mall
WB 36 " DO Something" Event

Teen Week Youth Rally
Make a Difference Day W/Cool Girls@Planet Hol-
    lywood
Check Yourself Live Broadcast
Marshall Newsome Food Drive
Boys & Girls B-Ball Challenge
AIDS Walk Atlanta
Marietta High Career Day
McDonald's Apollo Kid's Run
Living Legends Tour
CAU Bone Marrow Drive
Moreland Ave. Womens/Children' Shelter
Coca Cola Christmas Caravan
Clothing/Food Drive
Children's Restoration Network Easter Gala
Church's Habitat for Humanity
Planned Parenthood Teen Action @ Planet Hollywood
Ryan Cameron Celebrity Bowling Challenge for
Sickle Cell
Children's Restoration Network Mother's Day
Dinner
SCLC "Stop the Killing March"
Coca Cola Attendance Competition
Vote Jam@ CAU
Money Talks Tax Preparation Day
World AIDS Day at Spelman

Many of these programs and services are useful to youth. For instance, a segment titled "Money Talks Scholarships Tips" offers information to students regarding the proper procedure to find and apply for education scholarships. This communiqué airs in thirty second segments throughout the peak hours of broadcasting. In addition, the station has teamed with Coca Cola to sponsor *Attendance Competition 2000.* This competition encourages high school students to stay in school. The school with the highest attendance rate wins. Though community out-reach programs are notable and serve the black community, the play lists, target advertising, and marketing strategies undermine the politicizing of its youth audience. It is not unusual to see trucks or vans in predominantly black neighborhoods playing derogatory loud music (no politicized Hip Hop), giving away bumper stickers, CDs, free tickets and other promotional items to enhance brand recognition and listener loyalty. On any given day, radio personalities can be heard encouraging listeners to visit some location where live remote broadcasts occur. The problem here is that the majority of these locations are corporate retail chain stores. The marketing strategy is to encourage young people to visit these locations and spend money. Another marketing ploy disguised as community involvement entails the station visiting public school rallies, games and special events such as "theme week activities." Clearly an ulterior motive is to increase loyalty and new listeners.

Research also reveals that programming undermines the stations valiant attempt at outreach. While some programming is devoted to news, much of the news is of a trivial nature. Celebrity marriages, rappers' feuds and petty gossip enjoy more airtime than traditional news. The peak listening time for youth is from 6:00 a.m. to 9:00 a.m. during the academic year; in the summer months it ranges from 2:00p.m. to 10:00p.m.[164] The popular host Ryan Cameron enjoys a status that rivals the popularity of any celebrity. Unfortunately, his morning show *Future Flavors*, offers its youth audience little useful and instructive programming.

The process through which the station determines what songs will be played is also part of the problem. As discussed above, programming is based on market research, listener requests, and ultimately the program director.[165] Similar to its competitor, pre-selected pools of songs with no redeeming social value is available for listeners to choose from. Thus it comes as no surprise that listener call-in requests logs reveal that the majority of songs requested are drenched with didactic nihilism and materialism. Intellectual or culturally uplifting materials are almost never requested. For example, a copy of the WHTA request sheet which lists the top requested songs reveals that songs at the top on the list advocate illicit sex, drugs and violence.[166] The majority of the songs requested blatantly disrespect and dishonor women. More alarming here, is that young girls are the predominant segment that request these songs. According to Darrell Johnson,[167] the program director, complaints about the content of the programming are infrequent. Ironically according to Mr. Johnson, people usually call to complain about why the station is not playing these songs. Ultimately, WHTA is only slightly responsive to community concerns. The relevance for youth is temporal and no systematic political agenda is visible. Similar to its competitor, community forums, fund raising, outreach, and other charitable activities are undermined by irrelevant and consequently damaging music programming.

WVEE–103—The People's Station

Following a series of relocations, buyouts and changes in broadcast formats,[168] this station has become an Atlanta institution. Its slogan is "V-103, the People's Station." Its current music format includes of rhythm and blues, Hip Hop, and gospel. The station offers community event sponsorship and live broadcasts from locations within the community. Listeners are also encouraged to take advantage of services such as free as tax assistance, hypertension screening and a host of other useful services sponsored by nonprofit and government agencies.[169] With few exceptions such as "stay in school" rallies, such involvement is generally aimed at the black community at large but not targeted to youth.

In addition, the station offers several programs which extend a platform for community leaders, representatives of community groups and non profit organizations to advance their agenda in between music programming. For example, a radio personality named Frank-Ski has a morning program from 6:00 a.m. to 10:00 a.m. On this program subjects that range from local elections, technology, local controversies, international news and politics are discussed. The problem here is that most of these programs do not reach and are not intended for the youth audience who are in school by 8:00 a.m. Evening programming, from 6:00 p.m. to 10:00 p.m. and targeting the youth audience is drenched with advertising, loud radio personalities and music with expressions of devastatingly nihilistic music. The following analysis illustrates the point.

A program titled "Top 8 at 8" draws the largest youth listening audience during the day. The play list for the most popular program that youth tune into was catalogued for three days.[170] A sample of the lyrics of the most requested songs not only demonstrates that the programming has no political relevance for youth but also demonstrates the devastating impact radio has on advancing politicized HC.

The top 8 lists were comprised of some rhythm and blues songs which in many cases are just as derogatory as rap that advances nihilism. For example R & B songs that advocate promiscuity, misogyny and a range of other destructive behavior dominate the charts. One rap song which remain on the chart after six weeks, contains the following verse:

> I..f**k..these...hoes
> Af-ter...our shows
> Big d**ks... we slang
> Freak b**ch... do ya thang
> Benz, Vettes, Hummers, Jets Ro-lex... mo' sex
> Television... head rest Twenty inches... nothin less
> Every-day..... iced..... out
> N*gga play....lights out
> M... period... Fresh, comma
> Yo wife is my......baby mama
> God.......damn mother-f**ker
> She's uh....good d**k sucker
> What...the....f**k
> Hold on.....everybody
> Get yo' roll on.[171]

This pornography on record was the second most requested song and remained in the Top 8 requested chart for the previous two months and counting. Such decadent material is reflected in the majority of songs on the top eight lists. More alarming, such songs saturate the airwaves of black radio. Traditional civil rights groups, who are making waves about negative depictions of black life in Hollywood and network television, are virtually silent about this institution which shapes the normative ideas of African-American children.

Radio officials often argue that programming is contingent to audience requests. Considering the evidence, this argument is flawed for the following reason. Radio programming decides the pool of songs from which the audience chooses. As described, programming play lists are partly developed using lists complied by industry trade publications.[172] Most have no political or social redemptive value. The listening audience then chooses from the pool of records the stations are willing to play. To suggest that the public has impact on what music is programmed is mendacious and deceitful. Consequently, the assessment of WVEE is as follows. The station offers community outreach which encompasses a range of community concerns. Most of these come in form of announcements and bulletins. While pockets of politicized programming exist, few are targeted at the youth audience. The youth audience is simply targeted as potential consumer and customer. In addition, attempts at community involvement and responsible programming are sabotaged and undermined by programming bedraggled with didactic nihilism, materialism and a few radio personalities that would make defenders of *Amos 'n' Andy* proud.

Conclusion

The best advocate for politicized HC is community-radio WRFG. Some of its community outreach and programming not only target the Hip Hop audience but actively encourage youth listener participation regarding community concerns. The student operated station WRAS has possibilities, but non-systematic and sporadic programming remains a hindrance. The stations which advance politicized HC the least are the two commercial stations. Though sporadic social services are visible in the programming at both commercial stations surveyed neither have a definitive and comprehensive strategy to address legitimate concerns such affirmative action, education policy, police, and the electoral process, all of which are concerns of HC, who they claim to represent. In addition, their contribution to the perceived pathology of black youth has been virtually unchallenged.

Across the nation, the majority of black owned stations which do attempt to present some version of a vision for blacks are Christian Gospel stations. The problem here, as indicated in Chapter III's discussion about Christian Hip Hop, is that the majority of black youth are detached from Christianity. Thus even in the cases where the media is "black owned" and responsive, a general failure to politicize youth is obvious. A portentous opportunity is lost.

The term "black radio" is more a marketing tool than a reflection of any commitment to a political philosophy. Industry veteran Quincy McCoy puts it best: "Commercial radio has been about making money. Today the bottom line is even more important, especially to large radio conglomerate scrambling to pay back their Wall Street investors. . ."[173]

McCoy's commentary applies to commercial black radio as well. The real agents of socializing youth are not politicians, community leadership, teachers or gospel music; they are exposed to apolitical artists, often shallow radio personalities and the rancid apolitical music. The music is devoid of any residue of a political philosophy or cultural awareness. This is not to say that no such music exists, since HC clearly produces music with a political philosophy to which "black radio" is totally detached. One response to such detachment is the formation of HC's underground. The following chapter explores this subculture.

Chapter VI
UNDERGROUND HIP HOP CULTURE

To what extent Underground Hip Hop in general, and the Atlanta Underground in particular, serve as a viable instrument for developing and disseminating the liberating political philosophy must be examined. To be considered a viable instrument for propagating that philosophy, Underground Hip Hop, hereby identified as UHC, must not only lyrically reflect deference to the precepts of the philosophy but it must also advance counter responses to impediments of the development of that philosophy. These impediments, as discussed earlier, include didactic nihilism, spatial control and capitalist exploitation. Didactic nihilism has already been explained. Spatial control means the authoritative denial of access to public and private venues for HC activities. Capitalist exploitation refers to the appropriation of the financial rewards of HC production to the owners of capital as opposed to creative artists. Activities of underground communities in both the United States as a whole and Atlanta will be examined to ascertain the extent to which they satisfy standards for determining viability. Specifically, I will examine the lyrical content of prominent UHC artists with a view to determining whether they support or challenge didactic nihilism, survey efforts of UHC artists to secure access to public and commercial space and the response of authorities to their requests, and analyze efforts of UHC artists to disengage themselves from the dominant. Yet another challenge is to locate HC within the sphere of a relevant social science where investigatory practices do not merely mimic an irrelevant worldview but seek the development of new paradigms.

Consequently, this work would add to the body of information on HC by providing a theoretical framework with a political science orientation. There must be an expectation that if judgments about the political nature of HC are made, such evaluations should be made by political scientists and political science using political constructs. Although not only political scientists in political science are qualified to make judgments about HC's political elements, one would expect many more such analyses with political orientations to subsist within the body of literature. To distinguish between HC's positive and negative elements, recommendations regarding its political utility devoid of emotionalism and empty editorials *are* and ought to be, from a political science perspective. Standards, parameters, and a structural apparatus such as the constituent elements of a political philosophy allow us to distinguish between UHC negative and positive aspects.

Historical Overview of Underground HC

Students of HC assert that within the community there is a thriving subculture of autonomous voices independent of mainstream commercial HC. In the United States, this subculture originated within and is sustained by youth who suffer from the most extreme economic, social and political marginalization. Parenthetically it should be noted that there is an emerging international underground with documented communities in locations as diverse as Germany, Italy, France, Brazil, Cuba, and South Africa.[174]

In Cuba, for example, a derivative of Hip Hop called *Timba* has emerged. It is a combination of Hip Hop rhythms, political and social commentary and the religion of Santeria.[175] Similar to underground Hip Hop in America, it operates outside the mainstream popular culture. Ultimately, the case can be made that where mainstream HC exists, an underground also is detectable. In fact the underground is the driving force of HC's worldview. The Publisher/Editor-in-Chief of *Rapsheet*, a Hip Hop periodical, adequately described the present condition of UHC. In addition to its function as a political instrument,

> The underground of the rap music industry includes
> all of the artists who are creating the next new style

of music. It also includes, more specifically, the artists
who may be moving and selling large numbers of
units, but who don't get recognition because of not
being scanned properly. The underground is also the
hidden small clubs and college radio–the small cities
that the major labels often ignore.[176]

The origin of the term "underground" is not known, but
we know that the social reality to which it refers surfaced during
the 1980s as a response to the domination of HC by market
forces. Artists viewing the music industry as exploitative developed alternative modes for producing and distributing their
product. The underground quickly became an incubator where
striving artists congregated to hone their craft and sharpen their
political ideas. In keeping with the influence of NOI and NGE,
self-determination, black nationalism, and pan Africanism were
the dominant ideological orientations that conditioned their
political ideas. Underground artists responded directly to the
impediments imposed on them by promulgating a set of principles that implied both a code of conduct for HC artists and a
set of standards by which the music industry should be judged.

These principles proceeded from the assumption that while
artistic creativity is central to the future of HC, authentic Hip
Hop is the product of a lived cultural experience rather than
something manufactured in recording studios. Consequently the
contributions of rap pioneers must be respected. Commercially
successful artists, the principles also affirm, must remain loyal
to underground principles or risk exile from UHC. Regarding
the music industry, the underground subscribes to the view that
self-determination, including economic self-determination, is
mandatory. Black radio and other media, according to the same
principles, must become an advocate of politically relevant HC.
Talib Kweli of the group Black Star and one of the most popular
and respected artists of the underground captures the philosophy
in his work called *Manifesto*:

> One: First respect yourself as an artist
> If you don't respect yourself then your rhymes is
>   garbage
> Two: Make sure your crew is as tight as you

cause when them niggaz fallin off they gonna bring
    you down too
Three: Understand the meaning of MC
The power to Move the Crowd like Moses split the seas
Four: Know your sh*t and don't ever be blunted
If you don't know what your words mean then your
    rhymes mean nothing
Five: Kick facts in the raps, and curse with clarity
What's a curse when language is immersed in vulgarity
Six: We gonna fix industrial poli-tricks
Sh*t they made an artform out of ridin' d**ks
Seven: We soldiers for God needin new recruits
So if you rhymin' for the loot then you're a prostitute
    but
Eight: Acknowledge that you need food on your plate
In order to say your grace make sure your business
is straight
Nine: We buildin' black minds with intelligence and
    when you freestyle,
keep the subject matter relevant
Ten: Every MC grab a pen and write some conscious
    lyrics to tell the children.[177]

Clearly the manifesto serves as an indictment of artists who stray
from the principles and a set of guidelines for loyal adherents.
It is also a challenge to the industry and marketplace that are
viewed as predatory sources that often trivialize, extort and mis-
represent HC.

UHC and "Didactic Nihilism": A Response to Self-Destruction

HC artists and their associates who subscribed to tenets
reflected in the "Manifesto" were dismayed with the direction
taken by HC during the 1980s confronted the impediment posed
by didactic nihilism in a variety of ways. Some artists wrote and
performed lyrics that directly challenged the gangsta image and
themes of misogyny and drug advocacy. Indeed public response
to underground counter thrust was so positive that some of it was
picked up by mainstream outlets, confirming what Kelly refers
to as capitalism's "resilience and elasticity." The underground's

response to didactic nihilism transcended the actions of individual artists. Hip Hop artists banded together to set aside weeks devoted to positive projections of the community. Concerts and contests were developed to encourage and publicize involvement of the HC community in progressive social and political causes. The Atlanta UHC was especially active in such efforts.

Lyrics by artists such as De La Soul reflected the progressive political philosophy and unambiguously endorsed principles outlined in the Kweli "Manifesto." The first verse of the tune "Stakes is High" dramatizes this point:

> I'm sick of b**ches shakin' asses
> I'm sick of talkin' about blunts,
> Sick of Versace glasses, Sick of slang,
> Sick of half-ass awards shows,
> Sick of name brand clothes.
> Sick of R&B b**ches over bulls**t tracks,
> Cocaine and crack
> Which brings sickness to blacks,
> Sick of swoll' head rappers With their sicker-than raps
> Clappers and gats (guns)
> Makin' the whole sick world collapse.[178]

Verse three, expresses much of the same sentiment as the first verse.

> . . .its about love for cars, love of funds
> Loving to love mad sex, loving to love guns
> Love for opposites, love for fame and wealth
> Love for the fact of no longer loving yourself.[179]

The underground constantly challenges nihilism as an impediment to politicized HC. In fact, the Hip Hop community declared the week of May 15th to May 21st, 2000, as "HIP HOP APPRECIATION WEEK." According to one of its organizers "Hip Hop [K]ulture will fast from its criminal images to promote health, love, awareness, and wealth. Let us come together and show the world another side to Hip Hop."[180]

Hundreds of other artists including Common, Dead Prez, MAU MAU, Ran Reed, Mos Def, Black Star, Public Enemy, Pharaoh Monch and Goodie Mob have responded in similar fashion, attempting to counteract the mindless, spiritually void and nihilistic music that is commonly associated with HC. More important, these artists are central members of UHC and their ideas are shaped by the political philosophy outlined previously.

The response of the Atlanta Underground community mirrored that of the broader underground movement. Like the national community, the Atlanta Underground Hip Hop Culture (AUHC) artists covered the full spectrum ranging from apolitical to what some would consider militant. The more moderate artists who focus on lyrical sophistication, artistic creativity and positive political themes appear to be dominant. The more avowedly politicized elements, while present, generally lag behind other tendencies. Nevertheless, they are important actors in the AUHC. Many artists including one of Atlanta's most respected underground groups, Mass Influence, are associated with the idea of "real Hip Hop" that emerged as a response to the self-destructive tendencies within mainstream HC. According to one member, Cognito, the name "Mass Influence" is reflective of the ambition of the group to appeal to the masses and spread consciousness consistent with the Kweli "Manifesto." Like its national counterpart, the AUHC has organized concerts and contests specifically organized to counteract nihilism. For instance, organizers known as The Committee, holds contests called "Resurrection." Its main purpose, according to their mission statement, is to counteract "the lack of substance in commercial hip hop music and created an innovative format to challenge it." Other responses include organized concert fundraisers for journalist Mumia Abu Jamal, who is held on death row awaiting execution for a crime many contend he did not commit.[181] At these fundraisers several politically aware groups known within AUHC perform. Performers have included The Hemisphere, Jae Ellis, Vintage Imperial, Peas in a Pod, DASEAR, Vinyl Junkies, Bambu-de-Asiatic, Chief Justice and Old Souls. Similar to widespread UHC, AUHC struggles to counter didactic nihilism.

UHC and Public Space: A Response to Spatial Control

Much of the activity of HC's underground is a response to physical impediments; the denial of public space. This impediment is commonly referred to as "spatial control." In spite of

Nyack College Library

the freedom of speech guarantees of the Bill of Rights, the HC community has been forced to wage a continuing struggle for access to pubic and commercial space. Government authorities and the owners of private venues have repeatedly denied access to HC artists or severely constrained their creative freedom. Some scholars such as Tricia Rose have suggested that efforts to deny space to HC are part of the broader societal inclination to restrain and control black people. She argues:

> The way rap and rap related violence are discussed in the popular media is fundamentally linked to the larger social discourse on the spatial control of black people. Formal policies that explicitly circumscribe housing, school, and job options for black people have been outlawed; however, informal yet trenchant forms of institutional discrimination still exist in full force. Underwriting these de facto forms of social containment is the understanding that black people are a threat to social order. Inside of this, black urban teenagers are the most profound symbolic referent for internal threats to social order. Not surprisingly, then, young African Americans are in fundamentally antagonistic relationships to the institutions that most prominently frame and constrain their lives. The public school system, the police, and the popular media perceive and construct young African Americans as a dangerous internal element in urban America; an element that, if allowed to roam freely, will threaten the social order, an element that must be policed. Since rap music is understood as the predominant symbolic voice of black urban males, it heightens this sense of threat and reinforces dominant white middle-class objections to urban black youths who do not aspire to (but are haunted) by white middle-class standards.[182]

Spatial control is one instrument used to infringe on the rights of young blacks. More important, these youth attempting to counter effects of post-industrialism are denied public spaces to do so. One blatant example was the decision of New York's Mayor Rudolph Giuliani to deny a permit to the Hip Hop community to assemble at city hall to promote Rap the Vote, attempt by many in the Hip Hop community to register youth to vote and participate in the electoral process. Countless examples of spatial control have been documented; a few are listed below.

For fifteen years beginning in the early 1980s, block parties in New York City urban areas were routinely interrupted by police. Justification for the denial of public space was that city electricity was being used illegally. Fans and members of the group *Rage Against the Machine* were harassed at a Philadelphia concert by the Fraternal Order of Police in November 1999. The group has held fundraisers and concerts nationwide to bring awareness to the "Free Mumia Abu Jamal" campaign. Group members say they experience similar harassment in many cities while on tour. Graffiti artist Michael Stewart was caught by police while writing graffiti. Mr. Steward died in the custody of 10 NYPD officers. In 1993, *Rap Sheet's* former Editor-in-Chief, Darryl James, with other Hip Hop artists was handcuffed by police without probable cause. A few white friends of James ran out of the building with cameras. The officers took an apologetic mode and removed the handcuffs.[183] In 1997, Wu Tang members were detained and released shortly thereafter. According to police they fit the description of Bank robbers. In January 1998, one member of Wu Tang, known as ODB, was involved in a shoot out with NYPD. The case was dropped when it was learned that the police were the instigators and fired on the artist without provocation. In October of 1998, Method Man, another member of the group was arrested in Tennessee for signing autographs on the street. He was charged with what police termed disorderly conduct. Tu-Pac Shakur was beaten by Oakland police for jay walking in 1991. In 1993 two Atlanta sheriff deputies "mysteriously" opened fire on him and he shot back in self defense.[184] The case was dismissed when it was learned that the Atlanta police "encouraged" provocation. In May 2000, rap group Dead Prez, while performing in Florida, were harassed for exercising their first amendment rights by performing songs which highlight police brutality. The manager of the group was consequently arrested and released a few hours later.[185] Throughout the 1980s breakdancers on the Berkeley campus were routinely denied the freedom to dance in public. In January of 1999, hundreds gathered at a UCLA campus for B-Boy summit, an annual worldwide conference on HC. According to police reports, organizers had no permit to stage concerts on the beach at Venice. This led to a few altercations between police and attendees.

These incidents demonstrate the oppressive response by law (enforcement) to those representatives of the Hip Hop community who challenge America. These incidents also show how law enforcement power is used to deny access to public space to address their grievances. *Proposition 21*, described as an "anti-gang initiative," passed in California. The proposition among other things reclassifies graffiti (writing on walls) as a felony, requires supposed gang members to "register" with police departments similar to sex offenders, and classifies three or more people similarly dressed, as a gang. It is common that youth who identify with HC from similar and diverse backgrounds dress similar. Style similarity is a hallmark of HC.

While no specific response to spatial control has been located, activism seems to encompass a broad range of issues, most of which do not specifically address spatial control but reflect a reaction to it. For example, members of the Seattle UHC such as the Student Hip Hop Organization of Washington, Jasiri Media Group, and Pak Pros on several occasions protested the unfair media representations of HC, which promote fear of HC. This ultimately leads to the rejection of concert venues for HC based on fear. The Third Eye Movement from Oakland has aggressively and frequently sought redress from Oakland's law enforcement and its elected officials regarding police brutality and harassment. This protest is the result of a rookie officer's testimony that four fellow Oakland officers were planting evidence on suspects and falsifying reports. Other activities include campaigns by members of HC to help defeat the Juvenile Crime Initiative (Proposition 21), Anti-immigration Bill (Proposition 187), Anti-Affirmative Action Bill (Proposition 209) and The English Only Initiative (Proposition 227). While Propositions 187, 209 and 227 do not directly reflect the denial of public space, they do in fact impede access, which is the nucleus of denied public space. UHC has responded by addressing these propositions collectively.

In Chicago, community leaders joined members of HC to boycott venues such as, The House of Blues for not allowing Hip Hop artists and promoters to perform and use their facilities. These and other responses from UHC reflect a counter to the continued denial of public space.[186]

The denial of public space is also observable in Atlanta. There are "no cruising" laws[187] in downtown Atlanta that make driving on a specific street frequently and within a specific amount of time a punishable transgression.[188] Midtown Atlanta, now occupied by a majority of white middle class "urban pioneers," as they are frequently called, was first to post such signs. Such ordinances, until recently were not visible in Atlanta's predominantly black neighborhoods. The point here is that such ordinances are specifically designed to target black youth who tend to gather in these public spaces where the ordinances are in effect. Accusations of harassment of blacks by police in the Buckhead[189] section of Atlanta have surfaced. The issue found its way into the Atlanta city council where one council member, Derrick Boazman, remarked that his constituency "don't want black people in Buckhead."[190] In this case the denial of public space was clearly articulated. This racial dynamic within the city's most popular area seems to coincide with the escalated number of Hip Hop events and concerts in Buckhead in the last few years. Consequently, the visibility of blacks has increased dramatically in this affluent section of the city.

Tactics to terminate the annual The Black College Weekend "Freaknik," by closing off main arteries that lead into the white sections of the city, encouraging promoters and students to have events in black neighborhoods, and the presence of law enforcement in riot gear during this weekend are other glaring examples of denied public space.

Moreover, the majority of the Hip Hop concerts in Atlanta were held at a venue known as The Taberacle. The high number of law enforcement officials, private security and barricades would lead one to believe that preparations were being made for a protest against the World Trade Organization rather than a Hip Hop show.

AUHC has not *specifically* addressed any of the ordeals described above. The response to denied public space is reflected in the overall attempt at political organizing and mobilization of youth. For instance, a group based in Decatur, Georgia called HHPAC (Hip Hop Political Action Committee), is attempting to address the concerns of youth by developing a political base. According to the organization's founder, "As young, black people we know to vote, and that's all good, but we have to learn how to organize our political strength. My goal is to bring together the power of the hip-hop generation. To be vocal and effective, not only politically, but in changing our communities."[191]

The group operates similar to other political action committees. It attempts to raise campaign funds for politicians who listen to the voice and address the concerns of the Hip Hop generation. Issues such as affirmative action, police profiling and harassment,[192] education reform and job training are among the myriad of concerns to which redress is sought. The organization has gained the support of Hip Hop strategists such as Chuck D of Public Enemy, Professor Griff, and Afeni Shakur, mother of the slain rapper TuPac Shakur. In addition, several community activists serve as board members and advisors. Since its inception the organization's membership has steadily increased and its short-term objective is to raise $50,000 to $100,000 before the year end.

Another group that attempts to connect politicized HC's mission with the community at large is The Nation Time Syndicate (NTS). Founded in 1991, NTS's motto is "raising consciousness through Hip Hop." Its mission is to use HC as a tool to educate, empower and develop strategies to counter the damaging aspects of HC embraced by the popular society. According to its mission,

> We seek to bring a balanced view of Hip-Hop culture to counter the negative images that most people have been shown. We understand the importance of media and by using various media outlets; print, TV, radio, and Internet we are able to effect change

within our communities. Hip Hop culture as defined
by NTS is a way of life that has influenced almost
every aspect of our lives i.e. music, fashion, movies,
TV, politics, spirituality, language etc. NTS believes
members of the Hip- Hop Nation, are people from
every race, age group, sex, economic, social and
educational background that have an understanding
of, respect for and support the culture. NTS is dedicated to educating and enlightening the world about
Hip-Hop culture, history, accomplishments and its
contributions.[193]

NTS co- founder, David Tavares, hosts community forums that
address the development of political strategies, the direction of HC,
misogyny and a range of issues that reflect community concerns.[194]
The hope is that awareness will lead to engagement. Community forums sponsored by the group include, "Time + Effort =
Success," "Hip Hop History," "Lyrics, Hip Hop Stereotypes," "The
Impact of Videos," "Hip Hop, GOD & You," "Women In Hip
Hop," "Hip Hop Politics/Voter Registration," and "Poetry in the
Culture." In addition, NTS has a national and international focus
that attempts to link like organization and agendas. NTS also offers
online programming. Audio feeds of the three Hip Hop broadcasts
on WRFG are available at NTS's website, www.nationtime.com.
The network of community activists, artists and educators who are
members of NTS enriches its function and serves as a symbol of
HC's political potential to affect change.

The Atlanta Hip Hop Coalition has a similar mission. The
organization's mission is to create a united front of artists and
grassroots organizations that ultimately design political action
plans. For instance they are active in voter registration of eligible
voters, specifically youth; and co- sponsor fund-raising events
previously discussed. Though most responses to the impediment
of public space are in their embryonic stages, the attempt to seek
redress is exemplary and represents the formation of a post civil
rights youth activism.

UHC and Capitalism: A Response to Perceived Exploitation

The application of several economic models for explaining the black economy further illustrates one function of UHC, that is, to respond to the external and internal dynamics of the free market economy which often arrest and impede the establishment of a black political economy. Revisiting the critique of Donald Harris's colonial model as a conceptual scheme for understanding the economic conditions of black America is useful here. According to Jones and Barker, Harris concludes that the economy has a corporate and petty capitalist sector.

> The corporate capitalist sector provides a reasonably adequate material life for those workers employed in it. The return to workers in the petty capitalist sector is much less adequate. . . . The petty capitalists sector is made up of relatively small, often poorly capitalized, labor intensive firms with a low paid preponderantly non-unionized workforce.[195]

Black workers are employed disproportionately in the petty capitalist sector. Others such as William Julius Wilson reason that this disproportionate employment in the petty capitalist sector is the result of various factors. Wilson's thesis suggests that a structural transformation of cities and technology results in a changing economic order. This ultimately leads to the flight of the middle class and a decline in inner city jobs, resulting in social isolation and economic casualties, thus the formation of what is commonly referred to as the underclass.[196] Wilson contends that this social isolation leads to a rise in crime and social pathology. One response by Wilson's subjects has been self-employment. Free market capitalism allows financial benefits for some who have found a medium (HC) of (self) employment. Thus the cultural product of disillusioned young males that Wilson identifies as unsuitable for marriage offers an alterative to the petty capitalist sector described by Harris. UHC can be viewed as the incubator of these economic responses. Resistance to economic exploitation and obstacles created by post-industrial America is located in the most inconspicuous spaces, specifically UHC.

For example, elements of UHC such as graffiti, breaking, DJing and MCing,[197] represent a source of labor that generates income, inspiration and pleasure. According to Kelley,

> these strategies do not undermine capitalism; profits generated by the most successful ventures simply buttress capitalism and illustrate, once again, its amazing resilience and elasticity, even when the commodities themselves offer ideological challenges to its basic premise.[198]

Considering that HC's political philosophy is derived from the NOI and NGE, its economic ideas are similar. It is hardly a coincidence that many of the NOI and NGE members are central participants within UHC. The point made by Kelley regarding ideological challenges to capitalism's basic premise is glaring. While both organizations and UHC critique capitalism, the attempt to transform it has no structural focus. That is, the emphasis is on the eradication of white exploitation, not exploitation itself. It is widely accepted that neither NOI nor NGE advocate an end to capitalism. Their philosophy advocates replacing white capitalists with black capitalists as a precondition for self-empowerment. UHC reflects much of the same philosophy. The insistence to be economically independent and self-determined is one of the general aims of UHC. Thus, breaking the chains of exploitation leads many to self produce, market and distribute their materials minus interactions with institutions such as major record labels that have historically exploited blacks.[199] The figures below regarding rap sales illustrate a more accurate picture of the commerce HC has generated. More important, it reflects earnings in the hands of the "white custodians of black culture."

Consequently, independent artists within UHC position themselves to eliminate exploitation by stressing economic independence. The underground has developed a rudimentary economic system that is connected to the basic ideology of capitalism. Artists within the underground use concerts, industry meetings, college radio and the Internet to distribute their songs, advocate independence and push "Black Capitalism." Using information technology such as the Internet represents a recent strategy to

Table 4. Income Generated From Rap Sales[200]

Year	Sales
1991	$ 783 million dollars
1992	$ 776 million dollars
1993	$ 924 million dollars
1994	$ 1.19 billion dollars
1995	$ 825 million dollars
1996	$ 1.10 billion dollars
1997	$ 1.15 billion dollars

achieve and maintain economic independence and is worthy of closer examination.

A response to underground Hip Hop's commodification by the white music industry has been to remove the exploitative agents from the economic equation. New technology threatens to radically transform the traditional ownership and dissemination of culture.

Several technology firms have developed systems which provide access to music using a modem. Companies such as Napster and MP3.com convert digital music into compressed files that allows the end users to download music. Once download occurs the end user can save the file, trade the file, delete the file or repackage the file. Most choose either to trade or save the file. For the music industry in general and HC specifically, the ramifications are far reaching. For those artists in Hip Hop culture whose message is neutralized by the matrix of the music industry, this technology offers an alternative where products can be sold directly to the consumer. The tripartite system of ownership, censorship and economic exploitation of young blacks by major conglomerates such as EMI, Sony, Time Warner and Universal is severely threatened. The diagram below demonstrates how technology may radically shift the traditional relationship between producer, industry and consumer. The traditional model demonstrates the historical method through which culture production is made available to the consumer.

Figure 5. Comparison of Traditional Model and Alternative Model of Product Distribution

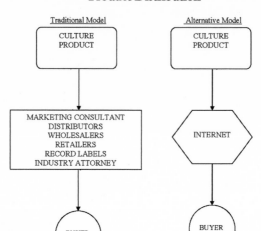

The alternative model illustrates a new paradigm that is quickly gaining momentum within HC generally and its sub culture.

The Internet is becoming the direct link between the public (consumer) and the artist. The threat to the industry has not gone unchallenged. Such challenges are reflective of the financial stakes. The companies listed above under the umbrella of the Record Industry Association of America (RIAA)[201] have all sued Napster, which has about 20 million users,[202] and MP3.com for copyright infringement. The financial stakes are high. According to a study by Wilkofsky Gruen Associates, revenue from music downloads will total about $1 billion in 2004, while revenue from the music sold in retail stores will be about $15.6 billion.[203] The courts have recently ruled in favor of the RIAA and forced Napster to police its users, prosecute offenders and charge for shared files.

Not surprising, Chuck D, veteran critic of the music industry, is leading the fight against the music industry. His group Public Enemy was among the first to provide MP3downloads to the public. He has even organized contest promotions to bring attention and support to Napster's legal battle. Consequently, Chuck D has developed several websites which allows artists to submit their product while maintaining ownership of their masters. Listeners can choose to purchase and support artists free of commercialism, market manipulations such as censorship, and general interference from the record companies.[204] His position on the matter is articulated in the lyrics of one song in which he asserts,

> If you don't own the master, then the master own you
> Who you trust, from Swindler's Lust?
> From the back of the bus,
> neither one of us control the fate of our soul,
> in Swindler's Lust
> This is to the blues people in the Delta
> This is for everybody in the 50's that didn't, get their
> money
> Little Richard gettin half of a penny
> All of the super soul singers of the 60's
> All the bands of the 70's on the outside lookin in
> All the people that didn't make a DIME off their session
> playin
> And even the rappers in the 80's and 90's still tryin to
> get paid,
> from what they put in, yeah.[205]

UHC at this juncture has not impacted the online market in any substantial way.

Another counteractive measure to perceived capitalist exploitation is to release songs independently. That is, self produce, market, and distribute records, tapes and CDs without interference from major corporate enterprise. This is especially apparent with the host of white labels that circulate throughout UHC. White labels are vinyl records circulated and sold in small independent record stores which support underground artists. Many of these white vinyl records offer lyrics containing aspects of a political philosophy. This is not to say that all white labels embrace lyrical content with social value, but many do. These issues notwithstanding, UHC is the crossroads where, political ideology, capitalism and new art forms converge to develop a neo capitalist network reflective of self empowerment.

AUHC follows a similar pattern, with many artists including Mass Appeal having created a mutli-functional business network called *Nonstop Musicworks*. Various business enterprises include a marketing and promotion firm, a clothing line, a website where much of their product is sold and a record label which allows self-production and ownership. Mass Influence's attempt to generate income while simultaneously spreading HC political philosophy with little reliance on mainstream institutions is illustrative of many within the AUHC.

Even artists considered militant share a similar ambition. For example the multi-talented Jamarhl Carlton Crawford, also known as "UNO the Prophet," owns his own publication services, is a columnist a Hip Hop periodical, a poet, graphic designer an orator and has self-published several books. His political philosophy often targets those with the mendacity to demean or degrade black culture. His political ideology is fueled by black nationalism and his aim is to promote "culture consciousness" and to facilitate "black thought." UNO's entrepreneurial spirit is a quintessential component of AUHC's attempts at self determination.[206] There exist hundreds of young blacks (mostly males) who are attempting to use art not only as expression but as a way to actualize self-determination, economic success and create a sense of identity. This is not to say that women are not attempting the same. In the male dominated world of HC, Salaah Swan aka DJ Boom Bip reflects an admirable entrepreneurial spirit. Swan works at radio station WRFG, a graphic design agency, a music distribution company called *Ear Wax*. She is a DJ at various venues in the city and also sells mixed CDs.[207] Her creations are heard on Chuck D's website, rapstation.com. This partnership and numerous others represent a clear indication that cooperative economics is visible in UHC as well as AUHC. Similar to the underground elsewhere, AUHC is comprised of industrious, ambitious and enterprising young black people. Such examples are clear opposition to, and distinct from, the nihilistic and pathological youth described by Wilson and others.

That stated, such rudimentary enterprises will be more effective and efficient if vertical integration occurs. Claud Anderson's thesis of vertical integration has some relevance for UHC. According to Anderson:

> In the concept of vertical integration, a single entity or group controls all aspects of the creation and sale of a service or product, including obtaining the raw materials, processing and manufacturing, then distributing, marketing and selling the finished products. Through vertical integration, the group that controls the raw resources and markets can reap the profits without sharing its proceeds with middlemen and others outside of the group. The group has the chance to take its profits or reinvent them in the business. Either way, it becomes stronger.[208]

Once UHC and AUHC actualize these processes, the response to economic exploitation and relief from petty capitalism will be more effective.

Ultimately, UHC responds to the three major impediments to a politicized HC and while rudimentary, must be considered a contributor to its overall political philosophy which consequently aids in the development of HC as a political instrument. The response to materialism, nihilism and self depreciation developed by apolitical segments and advanced by the corporate mechanisms is present. Regarding its response(s) to denied public space, there is much work to be done. Many of the political activities do not address these concerns specifically; general mobilization and organizing seem to reflect the most visible response. In fairness however, the strategy seems to be that mobilization must supercede all other matters of dissent. Most political scientists would agree that the development of a constituency or base is central to implementing a good strategy.

The denouncing of white capitalists and not capitalism, which is a major component of its overall political philosophy, is also apparent. Ultimately, the future vision for HC is located in its attempts to be politically organized through the development of a manifesto, activism and political participation. This vision for the future is also found in its reliance on new technology.

UHC concurrently serves as the hub which incorporates creativity and develops strategies aimed at economic independence, as it concurrently advances a political philosophy. The push for more political activism from the underground has pushed HC to the forefront of activism and political participation. HC's activism has radically increased in the past few years due in part to its grassroots elements located physically and philosophically in its underground.

Chapter VII

SCHOOL DAZE: PERCEPTIONS AND POLITICAL VALUES IN HIP HOP

Embedded in HC is a well-articulated political philosophy but to what extent do HC participants adhere to and recognize its potential political viability? What determines their basic ideological orientation and their perceptions of the nature of the American political system and their assessment of HC artists as political actors? More specifically, what determines the political orientation of HC adherents? Are they liberals, conservatives, centrists, nationalists or integrationists? How do they view American society and political system? Is it perceived to be egalitarian or class stratified? Are HC adherents trusting of the political system? Do they recognize any of the political values of HC? Are they interested or disinterested in the political potential of HC?

A survey of first year students at the Atlanta University Center (AUC) answers these questions. The AUC is a consortium of five predominantly black institutions of higher education, four with undergraduate programs: Clark Atlanta University, Morehouse College, Morris Brown College and Spelman College, and one exclusively graduate institution, The Interdenominational Theological Center. Respondents were selected from each of the institutions with undergraduate programs. Although a sample of AUC students does not insure absolute external validity, it is a fair approximation of HC adherents. Most of the first year students in the Center are between seventeen and eighteen years old, the age group targeted by HC oriented marketers,[209] and the AUC student body is geographically diverse with most states being represented. New York, California, New Jersey, Michigan and Georgia have the largest number of students enrolled, while states such as Hawaii, Maine, and New Hampshire represent the lowest figures for all schools.[210] The survey instrument was administered to students enrolled in randomly selected mandatory first year courses at the four institutions.

Table 5. Sample Size and Institution, 1998

Institution	First Year Enrollment	Sample Percent	Sample Number
Clark Atlanta University	1086	5%	54
Morehouse College	820	5%	41
Morris Brown College	1030	5%	51
Spelman College	507	5%	25
Total	3443		171

Ideology and Perceptions of American Politics

Before discussing the perceptions of HC adherents of the political significance of HC, it may be useful to determine whether they are political beings and, to the extent that they are in fact political beings, identify what ideological orientations they espouse. The survey results show that HC participants are politically conscious beings who talk about public problems with their friends. As the figure shows, more than 90 percent said that they did so. Fig. 6. conveys that issues talked about include elections and presumably politics, crime, race, drugs and welfare.

However, what is said on these issues would be difficult to conjecture based upon their responses to questionnaire items designed to ascertain their ideological orientation. Respondents appear to be more centrist than either liberal or conservative. For example, as figure 7 confirms, only fifty percent agreed that the government should be responsible for insuring that no American lived in poverty while thirty-six per cent disagreed and another fifteen per cent were undecided.

Fig. 6. Discussion of Political Problems

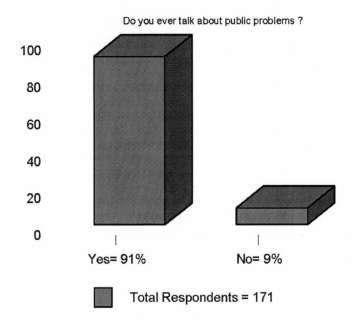

Do you ever talk about public problems ?

Yes= 91%   No= 9%

Total Respondents = 171

Table 6. Issues of Concern

Issues of concern	Total
Elections	44
Crime	22
Race	22
Campus life issues	21
Financial concerns	9
Personal Relationships	9
Drugs	5
Welfare	3
Rap music	3

Fig. 7. Government responsibility for eliminating poverty

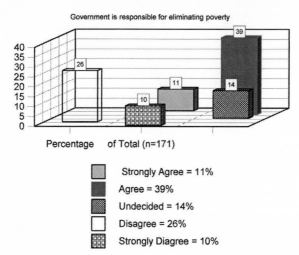

Government is responsible for eliminating poverty

Percentage   of Total (n=171)

■ Strongly Agree = 11%
■ Agree = 39%
■ Undecided = 14%
□ Disagree = 26%
▦ Strongly Diagree = 10%

As reflected in figure 8, twenty-six percent agreed that welfare programs such as food stamps did more harm than good while thirty-nine percent disagreed and thirty-five percent were undecided. These responses suggest more of a centrist orientation than anything else. However, on other items the respondents seem to be slightly left of center.

Fig. 8. Public welfare programs.

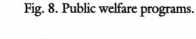

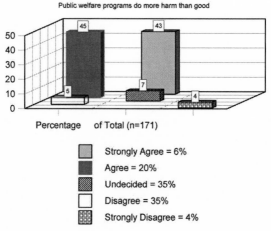

Public welfare programs do more harm than good

Percentage   of Total (n=171)

■ Strongly Agree = 6%
■ Agree = 20%
■ Undecided = 35%
□ Disagree = 35%
▦ Strongly Disagree = 4%

This supposition is supported by the fact that eighty-three percent of the respondents agreed that the political system is in the hands of wealthy people and sixty-six percent believed that government did not listen "to people like me."

Fig. 9. The political system is in the hands of the wealthy.

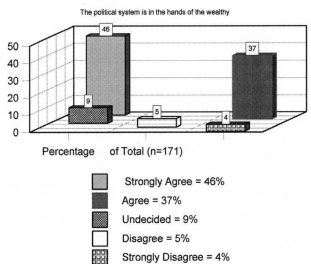

A majority, fifty-two percent believed that there will always "be a lot of people living in poverty" in the United States. These beliefs all have a liberal tinge.

With specific reference to the position of African Americans in American society, almost three-fourths, seventy-one percent, agree that slavery and generations of discrimination have created conditions that make it difficult for Blacks to work their way out of poverty.

Fig. 10. Generations of slavery and discrimination.

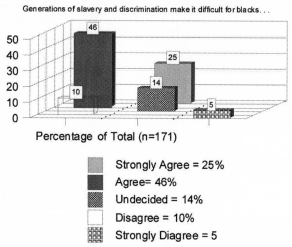

Generations of slavery and discrimination make it difficult for blacks...

Percentage of Total (n=171)

Strongly Agree = 25%
Agree= 46%
Undecided = 14%
Disagree = 10%
Strongly Diagree = 5

At the same time, as figure 11 shows, sixty-eight percent agreed that the interests of blacks could be best served by integration into the socio-economic and cultural systems, and eighty-eight percent agreed that the conditions of African Americans could be improved by running for and holding public office.

Fig. 11. Blacks can improve their conditions by voting

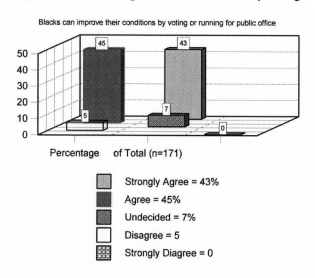

Blacks can improve their conditions by voting or running for public office

Percentage   of Total (n=171)

Strongly Agree = 43%
Agree = 45%
Undecided = 7%
Disagree = 5
Strongly Diagree = 0

These beliefs about the continuing negative impact of slavery and discrimination and the efficacy of integration do not necessarily distinguish between liberals and conservatives. Taken as a whole, however, these responses are clearly in conflict with the separatist, nationalist, African centered ideology visible in the philosophy of politicized Hip Hop.

Trust and the Political Process

Survey results show that respondents have little trust in the political system. I have already reported that preponderant majorities felt that the political system is in the hands of the wealthy and that the government does not listen to people like themselves. As figure 12 illustrates, sixty-one percent agreed that government officials are crooks and only thirteen percent disagreed.

Fig. 12. Government officials and Hip Hop artists.

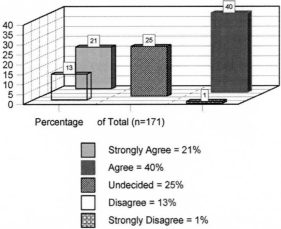

I agree with Hip Hop artists who say government officials are crooks

Percentage   of Total (n=171)

Strongly Agree = 21%
Agree = 40%
Undecided = 25%
Disagree = 13%
Strongly Disagree = 1%

When government officials are black, respondents show a greater degree of trust. As figure 13 illustrates, sixty-four per cent agreed that black elected officials had the power to help "black people" while only thirteen percent demurred.

Fig. 13. Black elected officials and power

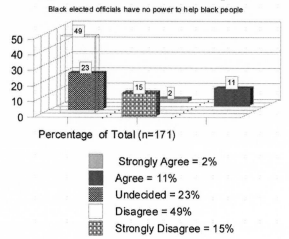

Black elected officials have no power to help black people

Percentage of Total (n=171)

Strongly Agree = 2%
Agree = 11%
Undecided = 23%
Disagree = 49%
Strongly Disagree = 15%

HC and Political Potential

This section determines whether participants recognize the political potential in HC and to what extent are they interested in it. Respondents demonstrated an awareness of the political potential of HC. However, they seemed disinclined to operationalize it. As figure 14 illustrates, sixty-six percent disagreed with the statement that Hip Hop music should be about partying and not politics, eleven percent agreed, and thirty-one percent were undecided.

Fig. 14. Hip Hop, partying, and politics.

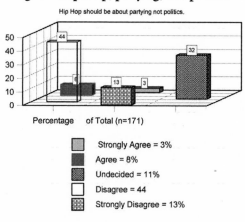

Hip Hop should be about partying not politics.

Percentage   of Total (n=171)

Strongly Agree = 3%
Agree = 8%
Undecided = 11%
Disagree = 44
Strongly Disagree = 13%

Seventy-three percent agreed that the political message of Hip Hop tunes was more important than the beat. On the other hand, sixty-six percent reported that they listened to songs about partying rather than politics even though only eighteen percent found politicized HC to be boring.

Fig. 15. Political messages in Hip Hop are boring.

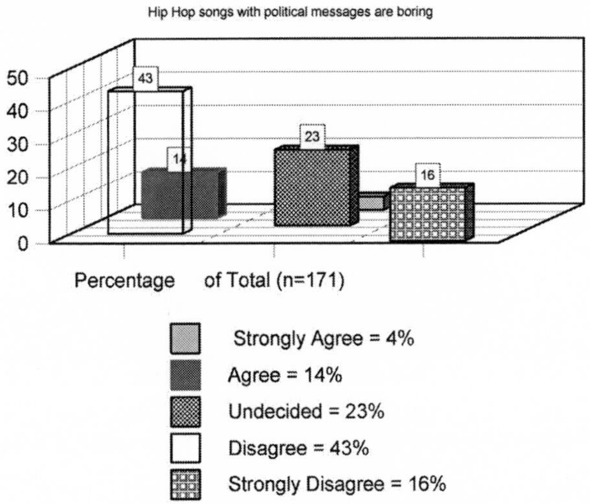

Hip Hop songs with political messages are boring

Percentage   of Total (n=171)

- Strongly Agree = 4%
- Agree = 14%
- Undecided = 23%
- Disagree = 43%
- Strongly Disagree = 16%

These results complement an earlier report on respondents' favorite artists that showed that performers who produced non-politicized music were preferred overwhelmingly over those who works were political. To extrapolate, while respondents recognize that Hip Hop as an art form can and should be a politically relevant vehicle, they show little interest in making it happen.

Respondents have a somewhat ambivalent attitude regarding the significance and commitment of HC artists as political workers. They were perceived as caring and generous members of the black community, but their artistry was not viewed as having a significant political impact on listeners. As figure 16 illustrates, thirty-one percent thought that their favorite artist was more concerned with uplifting black people than with "getting paid" while thirty-seven percent disagreed and thirty-two percent were undecided.

Fig. 16. Hip Hop Culture is about getting paid.

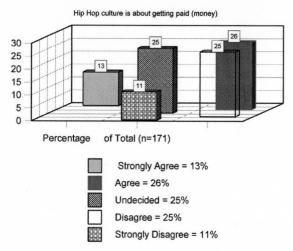

Strongly Agree = 13%
Agree = 26%
Undecided = 25%
Disagree = 25%
Strongly Disagree = 11%

Only eleven percent agreed that HC artists "don't care about political issues; sixty-three percent disagreed. Forty-six percent agreed that Hip Hop artists were aware "of important issues facing black people." A majority, fifty-four percent agreed that Hip Hop artists "gave back to their communities" and only seventeen percent disagreed.

Fig. 17. Artist and producers give back to their communities.

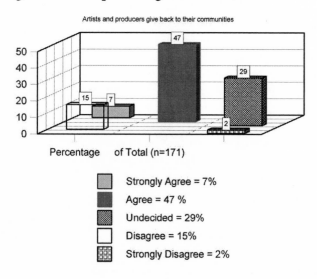

Strongly Agree = 7%
Agree = 47 %
Undecided = 29%
Disagree = 15%
Strongly Disagree = 2%

Regarding the political significance of the artistry, forty-six percent of respondents agreed that Hip Hop music helped them understand "the conditions of African-Americans," while thirty-eight percent demurred.

Fig. 18. Hip Hop helps me understand African Americans

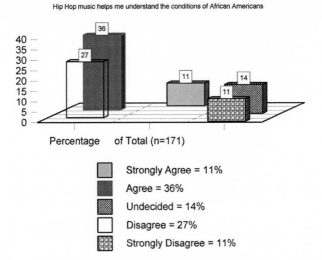

Hip Hop music helps me understand the conditions of African Americans

Percentage   of Total (n=171)

Strongly Agree = 11%
Agree = 36%
Undecided = 14%
Disagree = 27%
Strongly Disagree = 11%

Twenty-seven percent were motivated to join a political organization after listening to Hip Hop, but fifty-four percent experienced no such motivation. Similarly, thirty percent reported that they were encouraged to vote and participate in elections by the music, but a preponderant majority, fifty-nine percent said that they were not encouraged to participate by Hip Hop music.

Summary

The research survey reveals several interesting points regarding HC and the perceptions of its participants. While it is generally accepted by the participants that HC does in fact have political value, awareness of its specific philosophy is not identified. More important, adherence to the political philosophy is lacking. While Hip Hop artists are generally viewed as having great influence, most of the respondents selected artists who may be described as subversive to politicized aspects of Hip Hop. The impact of media, the failure of an aggressive political agenda, participants' apathy and the myriad of factors described previously all contribute to this inconsistency. While the data reveals that respondents have high interest in politicized HC, it is not reflected in their choice of music or artist. Lastly, there is low regard for the political process. Though there seems to be some recognition of its functional utility, it is generally viewed as in the hands of non-blacks.

Chapter VIII
GOVERNMENT MULE: THE POLITICAL SYSTEM AND HIP HOP CULTURE

David Easton's political system model can identify the procedures through which actors and agencies associated with HC function in the political system and the processes through which actors and agencies hostile to HC use government to monitor, regulate and control Hip Hop culture, while also analyzing the impact of HC on public policy.

According to Easton, the political system has three major components: inputs, outputs and the environment. Inputs are demands made by constituents, outputs are decisions and policy actions taken by authorities in response to demands, and the environment is conceptualized as the rest of society. Easton divides the environment into two dimensions, the intra-societal environment which encompasses the ecological, biological, personality and social systems, and the extra-societal environment, including international political, ecological and social systems. From these two environments inputs are converted into demands or supports which subsequently lead to outputs. Systemic demands made by the HC community as well as counter-demands made by its adversaries emanate from the intra-societal environment. HC actors have been more concerned with organizing and mobilizing black youth as a political force than with making specific demands on authorities for discrete public policies. On the other hand, the adversaries of HC have mounted concerted campaigns to censor and criminalize HC as an art form.

Hip Hop and the Shaping of Public Policy

Public policy is generally defined as a course of action taken by government. It is usually viewed as system outputs. Interest groups, political action committees (PACs) and lobbyists interact with policy makers in an attempt to shape policy making decisions.

HC's influence on policy outcomes is at best minimal. However, the failure of the HC community to gain concessions is not unique among groups championing the cause of African Americans. Limited or no impact is more the rule than exception among such groups. One reason may be income disparity. As Marcus Pohlman suggests, "Although technically open to every citizen, the input process certainly does appear to be more open to some than to others. For example, As Milbraith and Goel and numerous other analysts of American political participation have concluded, the poor spend more time eeking [sic] out a living, leaving less time for politics."[211]

Lesser status also makes the HC community less likely to have direct contact with the decision makers, while lower income leaves them less money with which to purchase special consideration by making large campaign contributions. In addition, the dominant American political value system may well be the leading the vast majority of American wage earners to accept their subordinate economic position as being apolitically irredeemable to economic injustice. Thus the political system may be far more likely to reproduce rather than rectify the inequalities of the economic structure on which it is built. Simply to ignore the possibility of such structural biases seems empirically myopic.[212] HC as a vehicle of disenfranchised people would obviously be subjected to the constraints suggested by Pohlman.

HC activists have been concerned primarily with organizing black youth as a political force rather than making demands for discrete public policies. By increasing voter participation and raising awareness regarding political concerns, the strategy is to put in office those persons who will advance public policy favorable to African-American interests. Three significant campaigns by HC activists dramatize this point: the Rap the Vote Campaign 2000, the No on Prop 21, and the Prison Monomorium Project.

The Rap the Vote Campaign 2000, organized by Russell Simmons, veteran Hip Hop activist and CEO of Def Jam, was a movement designed to register one million new voters and was specifically aimed at the Hip Hop community. A concurrent focus of the campaign was to make youth aware of policy initiatives believed to be inimical to black interest and motivate them to vote for or against candidates according to their position on the issues. One such issue was the bankruptcy bill H.R. 833 considered by the U. S. Congress in 2000. The supposed bankruptcy bill included unrelated amendments which among other things broadened law enforcement power. Simmons emphasized the importance of political involvement to youth by highlighting this as well as other machinations of some policy makers. Pohlmann's point is credible for Simmons has the financial resources to make contact with policy makers where most others do not.

Proposition 21 is a "tough on crime" California citizen's initiative promulgated in 2000 which authorized prosecutors to bring felony charges against juveniles aged fourteen or older without a judge's approval. In addition, it permitted the courts to sentence petty juvenile felons to adult prisons[213] and eliminated judges' discretion on sentencing by enforcing mandatory sentencing guidelines.

The "No On Prop 21" rally brought together scores of Hip Hop artists and associates, Oakland citizens, elected officials and clergy in downtown Oakland to attempt to sway voters to defeat the so-called crime initiative bill. The mayor of Berkeley, city council members, county supervisors and clergy from Christian, Hebrew and Muslim faiths were in attendance. Hip Hop artists such as Son of Nat Turner, One Nation Committee, Underground Railroad, The Black Dot Collective, and Third Eye Movement were central participants. Despite the steadfast organizing, California voters approved the proposition on Super Tuesday of the election cycle. The Prison Monotorium Project was another significant effort by HC activists that made demands on the political system. The project was organized to raise awareness and educate people about the current state of prison industrial complex. Professor Cornel West and a list of

Hip Hop artists produced a CD titled "No More Prisons," which they hoped would aid in raising public awareness. In addition, a forty-city campaign, which included activists training, workshops, conferences and performances by Hip Hop artists was expected to cultivate awareness nationally. The project was also aligned with several similar causes and is included in many concerts and events with similar missions.[214]

These efforts by the Hip Hop community to influence public policy are indeed modest. In fairness, however, such initiatives should not be viewed as the only indicator for determining its positive impact on community concerns. Political agitation is only one avenue through which community uplift and development may be pursued. Internally focused self-help activities such as developing cooperative businesses, conducting education classes, clothing drives and developing prison outreach programs are equally useful activities. HC groups routinely participate in such endeavors. [215]

While the Hip Hop community has not made extensive demands on government for programs that would address the pressing problems faced by black people in American society, it has been the subject of specific negative demands made by hostile forces. Such negative demands called for censoring and criminalizing HC.

HC's adversaries and the political system

Nihilism in HC legitimizes the need for reform. As described earlier, didactic nihilism and materialism in HC not only sabotage its positive utility but they offer ammunition to those who view black culture as degenerate and Hip Hop as immoral use the political system as a counteractive tool to regulate both. By failing to confront institutions and artists who perpetuate this negative one-dimensional portrayal of black life and culture, traditional civil rights organizations default on their responsibility and leave matters in the hands of those with ulterior motives. That said, measures that attempt to challenge aspects of HC using the political system are the most pervasive of the interactions between the political system and HC. Efforts to use the political system to challenge Hip Hop have occurred at the national, state, and local levels and they have involved forces both within and outside the black community. Moreover politicians have attempted to criminalize Hip Hop, and to demonize it in order to curry favor with certain segments of the electorate.

In September 2000, two New Jersey state senators, Gerald Cardinale and Diane Allen, introduced a bill that would make it illegal to sell any phonographic record, tape or

CD that contains lyrics which describe, advocate, or encourage suicide,[216] sadomasochism, rape, murder, morbid violence, ethnic, racial or racial intimidation and the use of illegal drugs or alcohol. It can be argued that American culture generally glorifies all of these assaults against humanity. This legislation was aimed at HC. Other mediums are not confronted with the same ferocity. A more famous case involved a group called *2 Live Crew*. In 1989, Florida Republican governor Bob Martinez used his office to send faxes to police officials and other politicians regarding the group's lewd material. He later asked the state's prosecutor to investigate whether Luke Campbell, the group's leader, was breaking indecency or obscenity laws by producing nihilistic music. A federal judge in Florida declared Campbell's material obscene and sales to minors were banned.[217]

In 1994, the Senate Committee on Energy and Commerce's subcommittee on Commerce, Competitiveness and Consumer Protection held a hearing. The subject was gangsta rap. C. Delores Tucker, head of the National Political Caucus of Black Women working with the GOP and Bill Bennett, forced the congress to address misogyny in rap music. Congress held hearings in 1994 with Senator Joseph Lieberman and Senator Sam Nunn as chairs of the proceedings.[218] Artists in other arenas were cited but the emphasis was on rap music. Although the Senate hearing did not lead to any specific anti-Hip Hop legislation, the public attention that it generated did induce a major record company to re-think its relationship with rap music. Prior to the hearing, Time Warner, an information conglomerate, was the principal distributor of Death Row records, the notorious producers of gangsta rap.[219] After the hearing, Time Warner ended its distribution agreement with Death Row. However, Universal Records, a Time Warner competitor, immediately agreed to distribute Death Row records through its subsidiary, Interscope records.[220]

On both sides of the aisle reform measures are used to gain a political advantage. Tipper Gore, wife of 2000 Presidential candidate Al Gore and founder of *The Parents Music Resource Center*, a group comprised primarily of the wives of Washington politicians, used Congress to force record companies to implement a parental advisory rating system in 1985. The overwhelming evidence used to justify the need for this rating system was extracted from rock music, but the majority of albums that display the warning sticker are rap albums. This legislation coincided with the heavy increase in rap music sales and popularity of gangsta rap in the mid to late eighties. Thirteen years later in 1998, the Senate Commerce Committee revisited the issue by holding a hearing titled "Labels and Lyrics: Do Parental Advisory Stickers Inform Consumers and Parents?" The twenty panel committee led by Republican Sam Brownback of Kansas also attempted to assess the effectiveness of parental advisory stickers. Using rap lyrics as justification for censorship was much more explicit. The committee invited a middle school teacher from Arkansas where an eleven and a thirteen-year-old killed four students and one teacher. The teacher, Debbie Pelley, testified that other students informed her that the alleged suspects habitually listened to the music of Tupac Shakur and Bone Thugs-N- Harmony. The implication here was that these artist lyrics may have triggered the murders.[221]

Former president Bill Clinton is perhaps the best example of how rap music and artists are challenged through the political system as subversive and used by political actors to consolidate a constituency. Months prior to the 1994 presidential election, Clinton used the words of an obscure rapper to pacify part of his constituency who believed he was afraid to stand up to Jesse Jackson. The scenario was as follows. Sista Souljah[222] in an interview in the Washington Post made a racial remark about whites. Clinton used her words to warn that hate speech cannot be tolerated regardless of origin. In the world of partisan politics, Clinton's ultimate political gain was that he echoed Republican sensibilities by being critical of black people and standing up to Jesse Jackson's coalition. The media presented Jackson as a defender of the artist. Traditional media pundits and Republicans frequently criticized Democrats for allegedly being reluctant to chastise errant blacks and stand up to Jackson.

Conclusions and Recommendations

HC is experiencing a surge in its political activities. Most activities focus on voting, especially in presidential elections. The recent voting drives experienced a great level of success registering new voters. Simultaneously, HC remains the incubator of black nihilism for adversaries in search of new Willie Hortons. Adversaries interested in baiting race traps and justifying their "moral values" agenda often point to popular culture and HC as a sign of society's decay. HC's failures to self-govern and chastise elements that undermine its political agenda will continue to derail any serious attempts at advancing its interests.

In order for HC to purge itself of those undesirable elements that undermine its political activism, a civil war must take place within the culture. Such revocations almost seem impossible considering market culture continues to advance these derogatory elements. Second, HC's political elites are relatively quiet on this point. When confronted, they point to the general society's decadence and suggest HC is merely a reflection of the general culture. Such responses reflect a refusal to confront the clash between didactic nihilism and political empowerment. More importantly, HC's political aspirations and activism become impotent gestures instead of proactive strategies.

Its negative aspects notwithstanding, HC is composed of enterprising and creative youth. Their attempts to forge economic and cultural freedom, develop strategies to uplift and advance Black people are too often dismissed. While scrutiny is a necessary component to identify control needs, success is as well. As countless writers have suggested, one consequence of being a historically oppressed people is the insistence that all that the culture of the oppressed creates is defective and beneath acceptability. One writer, commenting on Black achievement, puts it best.

> We may be the only oppressed people in the world
> who have struggled valiantly for centuries and sur-
> vived but have recorded no victories to commemo-
> rate and hardly any heroes and sheroes to celebrate.
> Rather than celebrate our victories, we seem much
> more predisposed to engage in none-constructive self
> condemnation.[223]

Incremental and progressive success ought to be a tool of liberation and not viewed as an aberration. To that end, elements of
HC that attempt to redefine Black life, seek solutions to historical
problems, posit the good about humanity, probe contradictions,
expose inequality, and shape a vision of self reliance must be supported and encouraged. In 1926, the preeminent scholar, W. E.
B DuBois offered a prophetic insight. He remarked:

> . . . we have within us as a race new stirrings; stirrings
> of the beginning of a new appreciation of joy, of a
> new desire to create, of a new will to be; as though
> in this morning of group life we had awakened
> from some sleep that once dimly mourns the past
> and dreams a splendid future; and there has come
> the conviction that the Youth that is here today, the
> Negro Youth, is a different kind of Youth, because in
> some new way it bears this mighty prophecy on its
> breast, with a new realization of itself, with new
> determination for all mankind. [224]

NOTES

Chapter I

1. William Banks, *Black Intellectuals: Race and Responsibility*, (New York: Norton, Norton and Son, 1997), 196.
2. Langston Hughes, "The Negro Artist and The Radical Mountain" in *Voices of the Harlem Renaissance*, edited by Nathan Irvin Huggins, (New York: Oxford University Press, 1976), 307.
3. Alain Locke, "Art or Propaganda" in *Voices of the Harlem Renaissance*, edited by Nathan Irvin Huggins, (New York: Oxford University Press, 1976), 313.
4. Tony Martin, *Race First* (Massachusetts: The Majority Press, 1984), 26.
5. Imamu Amiri Baraka, "Nationalism vs. Pimp Art", *Black Writers of America*, edited by Richard Barksdale (New York: MacMillan Publishing Co, 1972), 759.
6. Political utility used here specifically relates to whether AACP acknowledges, describes and presents solutions to contemporary political issues that affect the life and culture of America's Africans. These include issues specific to race, class, and gender.
7. Ibid.
8. Gordon Graham, "Book Publishing and Freedom," *Media, Culture, and Society*. (April 1993), 251.
9. bell hooks, *Outlaw Culture: Resisting Representations*, (New York Publishing, 1994: Routledge), 148.
10. Hendrik Hertzberg and Henry Louis Gates, "The African-American Century", *The New Yorker*, (April 29, 1996), 9.

11. Chuck D. with Yusuf Jah, *Fight The Power: Rap, Race and Reality* (New York: Delacorte Press), 185.

12. Ibid., 188.

13. Some culture products that are either too sexually explicit and/ or violent are sometimes "marketed" as underground, but not usually accepted by its constituents as such.

14. This refers to the representations of African-Americans as entertainment, criminal and poverty-stricken nihilists. These images are manifest in various aspects of American life. I contend that they exist in the majority of agencies of socialization.

15. Mack H. Jones, "Constituent Elements of Political Philosophies," African-American Political Thought, (Winter 1995).

16. Karl Marx, *Capital: A Critique of Political Economy*, ed. by Frederick Engels, (New York: International Publishers, 1967), vol. 1, 35.

17. Margaret Jane Radin, *Contested Commodities*, (Massachusetts: Harvard University Press, 1996)

18. David Easton, *A Framework for Political Analysis*, (New Jersey: Prentice-Hall, 1965), 57. Cited in Ronald H. Chilcote, *Theories of Comparative Politics: The Search for a Paradigm Reconsidered*, (San Francisco: Westview Press, 1981), 128.

19. Ibid.

Chapter II

20. Mack H. Jones, "Political Science and the Black Political Experience: Issues in Epistemology and Relevance", *National Political Science Review*, 3 (1992), 29. Jones references F. S. C. Northrop, *The Logic of the Science and Humanities*, (New York: World Publishing, 1969), 35-38.

21. Ibid., 30.

22. Lucius J. Barker and Mack H. Jones, *African-Americans and the American Political System* (New Jersey: Prentice Hall Inc, 1994), 9.

23. Pamela D. Hall, "The Relationship Between Types of Rap Music and Memory in African-American Children," *Journal of Black Studies* 28, no. 6 (July 1988): 802-814.

24. Other texts that repeat this theme are: Mary Ellison's *Lyrical Protest: Black Music's Struggle Against Discrimination* (New York: Praeger Publishers, 1989). Nelson George's *Buppies, B-Boys, Baps and Bohos: Notes on Post-Soul Black Culture* (New

York: Harper Collins, 1992). Paul Gilroy's *Small Acts: Thoughts on The Politics of Black Culture* (New York: Serpents Tail, 1993).

25. S. Craig Watkins, *Representing Hip Hop Culture and the Production of Black Cinema*. Chicago: The University of Chicago Press, 1998), 2.

26. Ibid.

27. William Eric Perkins's chapter titled " The Rap Attack: An Introduction" in *Droppin Science* (Philadelphia: Temple University, 1996), identifies Cab Calloway, Isaac Hayes, Gil Scott- Heron and, The Last Poets as Rap antecedents.

28. Russell A. Potter, *Spectacular Vernaculars: Hip-Hop and the Politics of Postmodernism* (Albany: State University of New York: 1995). A central thesis of this text is that academic discourse and contemporary art forms must make "vital connections."

29. A detailed assessment will be made in a forthcoming chapter.

30. Nelson George, *Hip Hop America* (New York: Viking Press, 1998), xi.

31. William Eric Perkins "The Rap Attack: an Introduction" in *Droppin' Science*, (Philadelphia: Temple University, 1996), 1-45.

32. William Eric Perkins, " Nation of Islam Ideology in the Rap of Public Enemy", in *The Emergency of Black and the Emergency of Rap*; Special Issue of *Black Sacred Music: A Journal of Theomusicology*, Jon Michael Spencer ed, 5:1 (North Carolina: Duke University Press, 1991): 41-50.

33. Ronald Jemal Stephens, " The Three Waves of Contemporary Rap Music. " in *The Emergency of Black and the Emergency of Rap*, Special Issue of *Black Sacred Music: A Journal of Theomusicology*, Jon Michael Spencer ed, 5:1 (North Carolina: Duke University Press, 1991): 25-40.

34. Maulana Karenga. *Kawaida Theory: An Introductory Outline*, (Inglewood, CA: 1980), 15. Cited in Errol A. Henderson, "Black Nationalism and Rap Music," *Journal of Black Studies*, 26 (January 1996): 313.

35. Errol A. Henderson, "Black Nationalism and Rap Music," *Journal of Black Studies*, 26 (January 1996): 313.

36. Ibid., 314-315.

37. Rose, Tricia. "Culture Survivalism and the Marketplace Subversions" in *Language, Rhythm, and Sound* Joseph K. Adjaye and

Adriane Andrews eds., (Pittsburgh: University of Pittsburgh Press, 1997), 263.

38. "Editor is the Only Black Publisher in Hip Hop," *The Indianapolis Recorder*, (June 21, 1997), b1. Also see, "Darryl James assumes full ownership of Rap Sheet; artists sought for Egypt Trip," *Billboard* 109 (24 May 1997), 28. James struggled to gain full ownership of a magazine that he started in 1992. He was successful in 1997.

39. Bakari Kitwana, *The Rap on Gangsta Rap*, (Chicago: Third World Press, 1995).

40. See Russell Potter's *Spectacular Vernacular*, 150.

41. Houston A. Baker jr., *Black Studies, Rap and the Academy.* (Chicago: University of Chicago Press, 1993), 98.

42. This thesis is repeated in works such as Doug Glasgow's *The Black Underclass*, Ken Auletta's *The Underclass*, William Julius Wilson's *When Work Disappears* and Jeremy Rifkin's *The End of Work.*

43. Patricia L. Rose, "Black Noise: Rap Music and Black Cultural Resistance in Contemporary American Popular Culture" (Ph. D. dissertation, Brown University, 1993), 47-48. This analysis is also located in chapter 2 of Rose's seminal text on HC, titled *Black Noise: Rap Music and Black Culture in Contemporary America.* London Wesleyan University Press, 1994.

44. Ibid., 41.

45. This point will be investigated in chapter 3.

46. Tricia Rose, "Hidden Politics: Discursive and Institutional Policing of Rap Music" in *Droppin' Science: Critical Essays on Rap Music and Hip Hop Culture*, William Eric Perkins, ed., (Philadelphia: Temple University Press, 1996), 254.

47. Robin D. G. Kelley, *Yo Mamas Disfunktional: Fighting Culture Wars in Urban America* (Boston: Beacon Press, 1997), 53.

48. Ibid., 46.

49. Ibid., 45.

50. Ibid., 77.

51. Ibid., 76.

52. George has authored several other texts on the interactions between black popular music, corporatism and the music industry. They include: *The Death of Rhythm and Blues, Buppies, B-Boys, Baps and Bohos: Notes on Post Soul Culture, Blackface:*

African-American and the Movies. In addition he served as *Bill-board Magazine* black music editor from 1982- 1989.

53. Nelson George, Hi*p Hop America* (New York: Viking Press, 1998), 27.

54. Ibid.

55. Ibid., 40.

56. Bakari Kitwana, *The Rap on Gangsta Rap* (Chicago: Third World Press, 1995), 23. Also see, Ronin Ro, *Gangsta: Merchandising the Rhymes of Violence* (New York: St. Martin's Press, 1996), 2.

57. This phrase is used to denote that most Islamic organizations founded by or practiced by African-Americans vary from those practiced outside the United States. While most acknowledge the general principles of Islam, many include what critics identify as racialist dogma.

58. Eric Perkins Williams, " Nation of Islam Ideology in the Rap of Public Enemy", *The Emergency of Black and the Emergency of Rap*; Special Issue of *Black Sacred Music: A Journal of Theomusicology*, Jon Michael Spencer ed, 5:1 (North Carolina: Duke University Press, 1991), 41-50.

59. Angela Spense Nelson, "Theology in the Hip Hop of Public Enemy and Kool Moe Dee," *The Emergency of Black and the Emergency of Rap*, Special Issue of *Black Sacred Music: A Journal of Theomusicology*, Jon Michael Spencer ed, 5:1(North Carolina: Duke University Press, 1991), 51-59.

60. Nelson uses one song by Kool Moe Dee titled "Knowledge is King" (Zomba Records, 1989) to support her position which is empirically insufficient. Public enemy on the other hand, has five albums where the majority of the songs are based in Nation of Islam theology.

61. *In Droppin' Science*, 159-191.

62. The forthcoming chapter attempts to present a detailed account of the relationship between theology and HC.

63. Harry Allen, "Righteous Indignation," *The Source*, 19 (March/ April 1991). Also see "Rakim: 5% Solution, Rap Sheet," (October 1992), 16 and "The Five Percent Solution" *Spin*, 6 (February 1991).

64. Greg Tate, *Flyboy in the Buttermilk* (New York: Simon and Schuster, 1992). Tate, similar to Harry Allen is among the first

to write about HC's evolution, politics and future. His earliest articles appeared in *The Village Voice.*

65. David Toop, *The Rap Attack: African Jive to New York Hip-Hop* (Boston: South End Press, 1984). Toop has also published a follow-up, titled *Rap Attack 2.*

Chapter III

66. Mack H. Jones, "Constituent Elements of Political Philosophies." *African-American Political Thought,* (Winter 1995).

67. Maulana Karenga, "Black Religion," in *African-American Religious Studies: An American Interdisciplinary Anthology* ed. Gaurade S. Wilmore (Duke University Press, 1989), 291.

68. This diagram was constructed by compiling the different variants of Islam developed and practiced by African-Americans from 1920s to present.

69. Clifton E. Marsh, *From Black Muslim to Muslim: The Resurrection, Transformation, and Change of the Lost Found Nation of Islam in America, 1930-1995.* (London: Scarecrow Press, 1996), 77.

70. Aminah Beverly McCloud, *African-American Islam* (New York Routledge Press, 1995), 28.

71. Interview with Ketema Allah (October 15, 1999). Much of what Katema Allah shared is supported by the historical record.

72. Articles appearing in *The Word,* vol. 1, (July, 1987), No. 1 (August/September 1987), No. 4 (October/November 1987) acknowledge these as the factors that may have led to his departure.

73. Ernest Allen Jr., "Making the Strong Survive: The Contours and Contradictions of Message Rap" in *Dropping Science* ed., William Eric Perkins, (Philadelphia: Temple University Press, 1996), 187.

74. Ibid.

75. Late night radio programs were pioneers at presenting Hip Hop programming. College radio stations and stations such as WHBI in New York were first to present Hip Hop programming. Listeners would call in to represent their neighborhood and acknowledge their friends by "giving a shout out." The overwhelming majority of the callers were members of the "Five Percenters" Nation. An interview with the DJ (Halfpint) of this late night program

revealed that he, as well as a few of his staff members were "Five Percenters."

76. Tricia Rose presents a detailed account of post industrialism. See "All Aboard the Night Train": Flow, Layering and rapture in Post Industrial New York" in *Black Noise* (London: Wesleyan University Press, 1994). Fred C. Shapiro's *Race Riot* (New York: Thomas Y. Crowell Company, 1964) and Jim Sleeper's *The Closest of Strangers* (New York: W.W. Norton and Company, 1990). These texts provide useful accounts of the challenges that face African decedents living in New York boroughs.

77. Thirty years later politicized Hip Hop still emanates from these same neighborhoods, suggesting that problems confronting black youth have remained virtually unchanged. These neighborhoods include Fort Green, Flatbush, Bedford Stuyvesant, and Crown Heights in Brooklyn. Fort Apache, South Bronx, Harlem, Jamaica Queens, Newark, New Jersey and a host of other communities within the Tri-State area. Currently, such problems have extended throughout urban America.

78. David Toop, *Rap Attack*, 58-59.

79. Brian Cross, *Its Not About a Salary: Rap, Race and Resistance in Los Angeles* (London: Verso, 1993), 160.

80. These are extracted from Mack H. Jones' definition of constituent elements. Statement of ideals, agencies, ideology and, ethic represent the other elements that collectively form a political philosophy. See *Definition of Terms* in Chapter One.

81. Elijah Muhammad, *Message to the Blackman in America* (Atlanta: Messenger Elijah Muhammad Propagation Society, 1965), 53.

82. Artists such as Askira X, Dead Prez, Sadat X, Poor Righteous Teachers, Paris, Ice Cube, and others express this theory in their songs.

83. Dead Prez, "Police State," *Let's Get Free*, (Loud Records, 2000), lyrics by Chairman Omali Yeshitela.

84. See other artists such as Common, Black Thought, Mos Def, KRS-ONE, and De La Soul.

85. Akari X for example. Title his album *Message to the Blackman* in honor of Elijah Muhammad.

86. Ernest Allen, Jr. "Making the Strong Survive" in *Droppin Science*, edited by William Eric Perkins, (Philadelphia: Temple University Press, 1996). Also see "Lost and Found Lesson No. 2" pamphlet.

87. See definition of terms in Chapter 1.

88. See Chapter 1.

89. Anne Campbell, *The Girls in the Gang* (Cambridge: Blackwell Publishers, 1984), 218. This list is confirmed by members of the NGE interviewed in Atlanta, Washington and New York.

90. Other albums by Brand Nubian include: *One for All* (SBA, Elektra) 1990, *Everything is Everything* (WEA, Elektra) 1993 and *Foundation* (Arista) 1998. These albums are deeply instructive and explain the political philosophy of the NGE.

91. Brand Nubian, "Dance to My Ministry," *One For All*. (Electra Records, 1990).

92. See albums such as *Being Myself,* (Warlock, 1999), *Solja Rags* (Cash Money, 1999), *The G Code*, (Cash Money, 1999), and *400 Degrees*, (Cash Money, 1998), by Juvenile, *The Life and Times of S. Carter*,(Roc-A-Fella, 1999) *In My Lifetime*, (Roc-A-Fella, 1997), *Reasonable Doubt* (Priority Records, 1999) *by Jay-Z*, and *The Block is Hot* (Cash Money, 1999) by Lil' Wayne.

93. See the works of artists such as Mos Def, Brand Nubian, and Dead Prez.

94. See albums such as Dr. Dre's *Chronic,*(Death Row, 2001) Snoop Dogg's *Doggystyle*, (Death Row 2001), *The Dogfather* (MCA 1998), and *Da Game is to be Sold Not Told,*(Priority 1998).

95. Notorious B.I.G., "The Ten Crack Commandments," *Life After Death*, (Bad Boy Entertainment, 1997).

96. The slogan "keep it real" is a rallying cry within HC. The slogan has several functions. It is used to critique lyricists who indulge in didactic nihilism. Second, those who express only materialist ideals are described as betraying HC and its political dimensions. Third, the use of the phrase is a scathing critique of artists who stray from describing the realities of street life, poverty, racism, police brutality, etc. It is a tribute and honor for a Hip Hop artist to be described as "keepin' it real." The slogan is used in the context of other slogans such as "the struggle continues," "keep fighting the good fight," "power to the people," etc.

97. Black Star, "Respirations," *Mos Def and Talib are Black Star.*, (Priority/Rawkus Entertainment, 1999).

98. Black Star, "K.O.S. Determination," *Mos Def and Talib are Black Stars* (Priority/Rawkus Entertainment, 1999).

99. Common "The 6th Sense" single (MCA/Universal, 1999). More outspoken artists such as The Dark Sun Riders, X Clan, Brother

J, Disposable Heroes of Hiphopcrisy, De La Soul, The Roots, Xzibit repeat similar ideals.

100. See *Definition of Terms* in Chapter 1.

101. Asadullah Samad, "Between the Lines: NOI's Cooperative Buying Program; Links Community Resource and Health", *Los Angeles Sentinel*, 3 March, 1999, A7.

102. Minister Louis Farrakhan, *A Torchlight for America* (Chicago: FCN Publishing Co., 1993), 84.

103. "Minister Louis Farrakhan establishing Nation of Islam political wing," *The Jacksonville Free Press*, vol. 12, December 12, 1998, 2.

104. Ibid.

105. Susan Sachs, "Muslim Schools in the U.S.: A Voice for Identity," *New York Times*, 10 November 1998 late edition, Section A.1

106. Minister Louis Farrakhan, "Message to the Hip Hop Community," *Final Call Online* (October 1, 1996).

107. Black Star, *Mos Def and Talib Kweli are Black Stars* (Rawkus, 1999). *Mos Def, Black on Both Sides* (Rawkus, 2000).

108. Online magazines such as *The Youth, The Five Percenter, The 14th Degree* and *Beyond* (a magazine for Earths) seem to be the direction that the NGE is taking regarding the development of its agencies.

109. The name derives from a lesson of the NGE as presented by Elijah Muhammad discussed previously. The "poor righteous teachers" are those five percent whose primary responsibility is to "civilize" the masses of black people in the wilderness of North America.

110. A more detailed account of this method of economic self reliance is provided in Chapter 6.

111. David Wall Rice, "The Vote Getter," *Vibe*, November 1998, 146.

112. Ibid.

113. See *Definition of Terms* in Chapter 1.

114. Elijah Muhammad, "The Making of the Devil" in *Message to the Blackman*, 103.

115. Aminah Beverly McCloud, *African-American Islam* (New York: Routledge Press, 1995), 60.

116. David Toop, *Rap Attack* (Boston: South End Press, 1984), 120.

117. Songs such as "Trans-Europe Express" almost fifteen minutes in length were accompanied by speeches. This offered the DJ a break and the opportunity to socialize for ten to twenty minutes. At the majority of these early gatherings that occurred during Hip Hop's infancy, politicized Hip Hop was broadcast using this method.

118. The term "old school" is a term used within HC to describe the first generation of Hip Hop supporters and artists in their teens and early twenties. It encompasses breakers, rappers, graffiti artists, DJs and fans.

119. Kam, "Intro," *Neva Again* (Eastwest Records, 1993).

120. Public Enemy, "Terminator X to the Edge of Panic," (Def Jam Recording, 1988). Farrahkan's voice can be heard on Lakim Shabazz's *Pure Righteousness*, (Tuff City Records 1990), Professor Griff's *Pawns in the Game* (Dead Line 1991), X Clan's *XODUS* (Polygram 1992) to name a few.

121. Public Enemy, "Fear of a Black Planet," *Fear of a Black Planet* (Def Jam 1990).

122. Many in HC have questioned Ice Cube's adherence and commitment to these articulated views. The content of his last two albums deviated from the former which gave him credibility among his peers. He is presently described as a purveyor of didactic nihilism. See Michael D. Clark, "Keep it gangsta," *Houston Chronicle*, 16 April 2000, 6.

123. Members include, Inspector Deck, U-God, Method Man, Ghost Face Killa, RZA, Masta Killa, Raekwon, GZA, Killa Priest, and ODB, all of whom are members of the NGE and openly express its philosophy on record, in interviews and, at concerts.

124. ODB, "Rawhide." *Return to the 36 Chambers – The Dirty Version Song*, (Electra, 1990).

125. Erykah Badu, "On and On," *Baduizm* (Universal, 1997).

126. See *Definition of Terms* in Chapter 1.

127. The name derives from a lesson of the NGE as presented by Elijah Muhammad discussed previously in this chapter. The "poor righteous teachers" are those five percent whose primary responsibility is to "civilize" the masses of black people in the wilderness of North America.

128. Poor Righteous Teachers, "We Dat Nice," *New World Order* (Priority, 1993). Other albums include, *Pure Poverty*, and *Holy Intellect*. Though Hip Hop culture dismisses Christianity, it is not uncommon for these artists to use Bible passages as a source of evidence to validate their worldview.

129. Nas featuring AZ the Visualiza (trumpet by Olu Dara), "Life's A Bitch," *Illmatic* (Columbia, 1994).

130. See "The persecution of the Righteous", *Message to the Blackman* Section IX and NGE's 120 lessons.

131. See Dead Prez, "I'm an African!," *Lets Get Free* (Relativity, 2000).

132. Goodie Mob. "Fighting," *Soul Food* (LaFace Records, 1990).

133. Boogie Down Production, "Beef," *Edutainment*, (Jive, 1990).

Chapter IV

134. Terms such as "Urban Christian Music," "Christian Rap," and "Holy Hip Hop" are also used to identify this brand of music.

135. Deborah Evans Price, "Christian sales see double-digit growth," *Billboard*, 21 July 2001.

136. Tom Lowry, Religion Rocks—So Sayeth Investors, *Business Week*, 10 June, 2002, 122

137. KRS-One, "Fourth Quarter-Free Throws," *I Got Next*, (Jive, 1997).

138. Joan Morgan, *When Chickenheads Come Home to Roost: A Hip-Hop Feminist Breaks it Down* (Simon & Schuster, 2000), 124.

139. Michael Eric Dyson. *Reflecting Black* Minneapolis: University of Minnesota Press, 1993), 323

140. Ibid.

Chapter V

141. WVEE (97.5- FM) and WHTA (103.5 FM). WVEE has changed frequency location and it is now at 107 FM.

142. WRFG: Community Radio (89.3 FM) and Georgia State University radio, WRAS FM- 88.5)

143. Louis Cantor's *Wheelin' on Beale* (New York: Pharos Books, 1992), chronicles the events and circumstances that resulted in WDIA becoming the first station in the 1 950s to have all of its programming specifically for African Americans.

144. Fred J. McDonald, *Don't Touch That Dial! Radio Programming in American Life, 1920- 1960* (Chicago: Nelson Hall, 1986), 327- 370. Cited in Gilbert A. Williams's *Legendary Pioneers of Black Radio* (Connecticut: Praeger Publishers, 1998), 12.

145. According to its mission statement, the MTDP was established to develop programs and policies to increase minority ownership in the broadcast and telecommunications, established in 1978 as a part of the National Telecommunications and Information Administration to develop programs and policies that increase minority and women-owned telecommunications businesses.

146. Since the report, Radio One has acquired a total of fifteen stations. See Robin D. Clarke's "High Frequency Profits," *Black Enterprise*, (June 2000), 130-136. Radio One's Press release dated June 9, 2000 reports ownership of 50 radio stations, 36 of which are located in 14 of the 20 largest African-American markets and 49 of which are located in 18 of the 40 largest African-American markets in the United States.

147. The research indicates that diversity of programming does not necessarily serve the interest of black people. This point is verified in the case studies.

148. Cited in U.S. Department of Commerce, National Telecommunications and Information Administration. Minority Telecommunications Development Program "Minority Commercial Broadcasting Ownership in The United States," 1997-1998. Since the release of the Commission's Staff Study, Chancellor Media announced that it Will merge with Capstar Broadcasting, the second and fourth largest revenue generating radio station groups, respectively. If the Chancellor/Capstar merger is approved, Chancellor will be both the largest station group as measured both by licenses controlled and revenue generated.

149. John Templeton, "Down to business about Black-owned radio stations," *Chicago Citizen*, 18 October1997, 24.

150. WRFG's mission statement.

151. Interview with station interim general manager Ebon Dooley, WRFG, Atlanta, (January 10, 2000).

152. This event, also called "Black College Spring Break" has been one of Atlanta's major problems. It has exacerbated tensions between elected officials, community leaders, students and law enforcement.

153. Interview with IRAS May 1, 2000, WRFG studios Atlanta. Several interviews with staff, guests and callers were conducted between October 1999 and May 2000.

154. In September 1999 *Nightline* presented a week long series on HC. The program enforced every cliché imaginable and offered nothing beyond white America's phobias and stereotype of HC.

Nightline a year later did a report on segregated proms in Georgia and did not make the connection that multi-cultural Hip Hop could not transcend the segregationist ideas of both black and white students.

155. See George's "Black Owned?" in *Hip Hop America.*

156. Interview with J Force WRFG radio show host, Atlanta Georgia, May 26, 2000.

157. Interview conducted with John Bennett, February 22, 2000.

158. According to Bennett, "safe harbor hours" allow such questionable material to be aired. These safe hours are between 10:00 pm to 6:00 am. He points out that most hosts choose not to air objectionable material by choice. In addition, the National Federation of Community Broadcasters (NFCB) sets guidelines regarding underwriting, programming and non commercial radio standards.

159. http://www.arbitron.com/aa.htm.

160. *Forbes* magazine estimated that *No Limit* CEO Master P, was worth 59 million, placing, him 10th on the list of highest paid entertainers in 1998. Also see, "Pushing the Limit," *Times-Picayune,* 11 June 2000, A01.

161. See *Getaway Clean,* (No Limit Records, 1998), *Mama's Bad Boy,* (No Limit Records, 1998), *Ghetto's Trying To Kill Me,* (Priority Records, 1995), *99 Ways to Die,* (Priority, 1995) *Ice Cream Man,* (Priority 1996) *Ghetto D,* (Priority 1997) *MP Da Last Don, vol.1 & 2* (Priority Records, 1998). All of these albums are saturated with didactic nihilism.

162. Source: SoundScan cited in *Industry Report,* www.industryreport.com

163. "Smile, drivers, you're on Mobiltrak," *The Atlanta Journal-Constitution* 1 December 1999, d3.

164. The morning show, targeted at this segment of black youth, is the most popular show and enjoys the largest market share. Though school begins for most students at 8:00 a.m., the ratings remain high until 9:00 a.m.

165. Potential songs for air play are sent to a media research firm (Strategic Media). The "hook" or catchy part of a song, is heard by a sample pool. A determination of the audience's ability to remember the catchy hook is calculated. It is more likely that a song with a catchy hook will enjoy air play because the youth audience will

identify with the hook, and ultimately tune in to repetitively hear the song.

166. This chart is categorized by the number of requests for each song, male or female, and the age groups which make such requests. Not surprising, the ages group that request these songs are between twelve and twenty four. Females between the ages of twelve and seventeen are usually the largest segment. This chart was dated 7/24/00. In addition, data such as listener profiles and a content analysis were gathered by listening to these programs for four two week increments. Listeners were asked their name, age, and neighborhood. The majority of the callers were female and that they all requested songs saturated with didactic nihilism.

167. Interviews were conducted with Darrell Johnson (Program Director), Twana James (News Director), Dimitrius McNeil (Programming Assistant), and Dwan Johnson (Sales Assistant) and several others during the week in July 2000.

168. The station started playing popular music and news in the 1960's, progressive rock in the 1960, disco in 1976 and by the 1980's urban contemporary, which is its current format.

169. The station supports programs such as the Forth Annual Women's HIV Healing retreat, part of the *Aids Survival Project*, The Giving Tree Adoption Agency's *Adoptive Parent Training (MAPP)*, and Operation *P.E.A.C.E.*, a non profit organization that aids low income families. A campaign to register voters throughout the Atlanta area has had some success.

170. The sample dates were April 28, 2000, May 29, 2000, and June 20, 2000. These dates were spaced to ensure a wide variety of data.

171. Big Tymers, "Get Your Roll On," *I Got That Work.* (Universal, 2000).

172. Many of those interviewed for this research indicated that "payola" is another determinant of the radio personalities playlist. Payola is an indiscriminate illegal payment offered to DJ's by record companies' executives to encourage them to include a specific song. The majority of the radio employees interviewed indicated that while they did not participate and do not condone it, the practice is still exists and is widespread.

173. Quincy McCoy, *No Static: A guide to Creative Radio Programming* (San Francisco: Miller Freeman Books, 1999), 3.

Chapter VI

174. Kwaku, "A global look at indigenous hip-hop," *Billboard*, 13 Nov 1999, 27-28.

175. Chuy Varela, "Cuban Gems / Voice of Discontent: Timba, like American hip- hop is new form of expression on the streets," *San Francisco Chronicle* 19 September 1999, 38.

176. Interview No.3 with Daryl James, Editor-in- Chief of *Rap Sheet*, Atlanta (May 20, 2000).

177. Talib Kweli "Manifesto," *Reflection Eternal*, (Rawkus, 2002) and *Lyricist Lounge - Volume One*, Priority/Rawkus, 1999).

178. De La Soul, "Stakes is High," *Stakes is High* (Tommy Boy, 1996). "Blunts" is a term used to describe the nihilistic behavior of smoking marijuana wrapped in a tobacco leaf. Its use was magnified by the world famous Snoop Dogg and Dre's Album titled *Chronic*, which is also another word used to describe marijuana.

179. Ibid.

180. See www.daveyd.com, article titled "A special message from KRS-ONE," May 15, 2000, 8:05 a.m.

181. This seems to be a popular cause. In the last year, I have witnessed eight such fund- raisers by Hip Hop organizations in Atlanta. Such concerts coincide and compliment other similar political event such as the *Free Mumia Campaign*, and *Fight Against Police Brutality*.

182. Tricia Rose, "Hidden Politics: discursive and institutional policing of rap music" in *Droppin' Science*, ed. William Eric Perkins, (Philadelphia: Temple University Press, 1996), 237.

183. James in an earlier interview stated this was a clear case of police harassment. The two rappers he was interviewing at the time were afraid to pursue the case for fear of reprisal from the police department.

184. Bill Montgomery, "2 in shootout once had fight with Shakur," *The Atlanta Journal and Constitution* February 1997, b07.

185. Members of the black nationalist group Dead Prez performed a song titled "Cop Shot." The song was a response to the Amadou Diallo case in which an unarmed African man was besieged by New York police and fired upon forty one times.

186. Chapter VII will present a more detailed account of these activities.

187. No cruising laws are laws designed to deter motorists from driving repeatedly along streets with not apparent destination except to cruise (drive slow playing music) along main arteries.

Youth cruise along these public roads as a form of socialization. The justification for such laws is that it creates traffic jams and those penalties and fines would deter cruising.

188. These signs appeared prior to the Black College Weekend "Freak-nik" in Atlanta in 1998. Black College Weekend is an annual event where black college students and others gather in Atlanta for spring break celebrations. Activities include parties, job fairs and public health campaigns.

189. Buckhead is a section of Atlanta described as "the place to be" for dining and partying. It is also identified by some sources as affluent. Tourists to the city are often herded to this section to town.

190. Stacey Shelton, "Racial talk about Buckhead assailed," *The Atlanta Journal Constitution* ,on-line archives (09/07/00).

191. Lance Johnson, "From the turntables to the ballot box," Black-politics.com.

192. The general category of harassment encompass the specific issue of denied public space.

193. Mission statement of NTS made available by offered by David Tavares.

194. These community forums are held once a month at the Atlanta Auburn Research Library.

195. Lucius Barker and Mack H. Jones, *African Americans and the Political System* (New Jersey: Prentice Hall, 1994), 11.

196. Economist John Kain and John Kasarda's *Spacial Mismatch Theory* echoes a similar characterization. Also see William A. Darity and Samuel L. Myers, *The Black Underclass: Critical Essays on Race and Unwantedness* (New York: Garland Publishing, 1994), 47.

197. DJing, pronounced *dee-jaying*, is considered an art form which entails the manipulations of music using turntables and other equipment. MC is an abbreviation for Microphone Controller and Master of Ceremony. It embodies the interactions between the performer and audience such as call and response. MCs or *emcees*, as it is commonly written, includes the lyricist, rapper or wordsmith. Both elements are central components of HC.

198. Kelley, *Yo' Mama's disFUNKtional*, 45- 46.

199. See Nelson George's *The Death of Rhythm and Blues* (New York: Pantheon Books, 1991) and Mark Anthony Neal's *What the Music Said* (New York: Routledge Press, 1998).

200. Recording Industry Association of America. These figures include black owned labels that most often are subsidiaries of the major music conglomerates owned by non-blacks.

201. Among these are EMI Recorded Music, Seagram's Universal Music Group, EMI and Sony Music.

202. Keith Alexander, "Top music sellers go online to fight free providers," *USA TODAY*, 18 July 2000, 1B.

203. Ibid.

204. See rapstation.com, publicenemy.com and, bringthenoise.com, which posts slogans such as "you control the technology, don't let the technology control you" are posted.

205. Public Enemy, "Swindler's Lust," *There's a Poison Goin On.*, (Atomic Pop, 2000).

206. See www.prophecycommunications.com.

207. Mixed CD's are sold throughout the underground. They are produced by various DJs who sell them on the street, college campuses, and underground venues such as small record shops, clubs, street fairs and the Internet. Recently, major labels acknowledging the profit potential have released several mixed CDs.

208. Claud Anderson. *Black Labor, White Wealth* (Maryland: Duncan & Duncan Publishers, 1994), 208.

Chapter VII

209. See Arbitron and Nielsen rating reports. These reports use several age segments which include this sample range. The Interdenominational Theological Center was not included in this survey for the graduate students are older than the demographic age profile.

210. This is according to the enrollment figures from all four colleges.

Chapter VIII

211. Pohlmann references Lester Millbraith and M.L. Goel, *Political Participation* (Chicago: Rand McNally, 1977), 97. Also see Sidney Verba and Norman Nie, *Participation in America* (Harper & Row, 1972), chapter 20.

212. Marcus D. Pohlmann, *Black Politics in Conservative America*, (New York: Longman, 1990), 21.

213. John J. Dilulio Jr, "Young and deadly," *National Review* (April 3, 2000), 28- 29.

214. See Rashaun Hall's, "Hip Hop Raises Awareness at NYC Black August Benefit," *Billboard On Line Magazine*, 31 August 2000.

215. Jon Caramanica, "Institution building," *The Village Voice*; 7 September 1999, 45.

216. While suicide is not a theme expressed in nihilistic Hip Hop, several artists including the late Notorious B.I.G and TuPac Shakur (both were slain), often talked about being ready to die and dying recklessly. Many believe that both provoked their death through their songs, which is viewed as an act of suicide.

217. Among those who came to Campbell's defense was Harvard professor Henry Louis Gates. Professor Gates testified in court that this form of music has long been a part of the African-American tradition of signifying. Gates wrote a book on the subject called *Signifying Monkey*, (Oxford University Press, 1989).

218. Congress, Senate, Subcommittee on Oversight of Government Management, Restructuring, and the District of Columbia of the Committee on Governmental Affairs, *Music Violence: How Does it Affect our Children*, 105th Cong., 1st Sess., 6 November 1997.

219. *Hip Hop America*, 190.

220. Steve Stolder ,"Aren't stickers enough?" *Rolling Stone* (November 2, 1995), 20.

221. Bill Holland, "Senate hearing reopens lyrics debate," *Billboard*, (June 27, 1998), 10.

222. The use of this artist as a target serves several other functions. Sista Souljah aligned herself with Louis Farrakhan and the rap group Public Enemy which Jewish people label anti-Semitic. Clinton's remarks would serve to satisfy the Jewish constituency as well.

223. Mack H. Jones, "Limitations of the Civil Rights Philosophy and Agenda: A different Perspective," Department of Political Science, Clark Atlanta University. Remarks delivered to the Twentieth Annual Black Studies Conference, Olive Harvey College, Illinois, April 14-19, 1997.

224. Eric J. Sundquist ed., *The Oxford W.E.B. DuBois Reader*, (New York: Oxford University Press, 1996), 326. Originally published as "Criteria of Negro Art", *The Crisis*, 32 (October 1926)

WORKS CITED

Allen, Harry. "The Political Proclamation of Hip Hop Music." *The Black Collegian.* Vol. 20, no.4, (March/April 1990), p 21.

Anderson, Claud. *Black Labor, White Wealth.* Maryland: Duncan and Duncan, Inc., 1994.

Attali, Jacques. *Noise: The Political Economy of Music.* Minneapolis University of Minnesota Press, 1989.

Babbie, Earl. *The Practice of Social Science* Research. California: Wadsworth Publishing Company, 1983.

Baker, Houston A., Jr., *Black Studies, Rap and the Academy.* Chicago: University of Chicago Press, 1993.

Banks, William. *Black Intellectuals: Race and Responsibility.* New York: Norton, Norton and Son, 1997.

Banner-Haley, Charles T. T*he Fruits of Integration: Black Middle-Class Ideology and Culture, 1960-1990.* Mississippi: University Press of Mississippi, 1994.

Bell, Daniel. *The Cultural Contradictions of Capitalism.* New York: Basic Books Inc, Publishers, 1976.

Cobb, William Jelani, "The Evolution of Hip-Hop" *Emerge,* (October 1998).

Costello, Mark. *Signifying Rappers: Rap and Race in The Urban Present.* New York: Ecco Press, 1990.

Cross, Brian. *It's Not About a Salary: Rap, Race and Resistance in Los Angeles.* London: Verso, 1993.

Cruse, Harold. *Crisis of the Negro Intellectual.* New York: Quill Press, 1967.

Dyson, Michael E. *Race Rules: Navigating the Color Line.* New York: Addison-Wesley Publishing Company, Inc., 1996.

Dyson, Michael Eric. *Reflecting Black.* Minneapolis: University of Minnesota Press, 1993.

El-Amin, Mustafa. *The Religion of Islam and the Nation of Islam: What Is the Difference?* Newark: El-Amin Productions, 1991.

Ellison, Mary. *Lyrical Protest: Black Music's Struggle Against Discrimination.* New York: Praeger Publishers, 1989.

Fauset, Arthur H. *Black Gods of the Metropolis.* Philadelphia: University of Pennsylvania, 1971.

Gates, Henry L. "The African American Century," *The New Yorker.* April 29, 1996, pp. 6-9.

George, Nelson. *hip hop america.* New York: Viking Penguin, 1998.

_____. "Rap Culture, the Church, and American Society." *Black Sacred Music* 6:1 (1992), 269-273.

_____. *Buppies, B-Boys, Baps and Bohos: Notes on Post-Soul Black Culture.* New York: Harper Collins, 1992.

_____. *hip hop America.* New York: Viking Press, 1998.

Gilroy, Paul. *Small Acts: Thoughts on The Politics of Black Culture.* New York: Serpents Tail, 1993.

Gottehrer, Barry. *The Mayor's Man.* Doubleday & Company, Inc, 1975.

Graham, Gordon. "Book Publishing and Freedom," *Media, Culture and Society.* April 1993.

Gwaltney, John Langston. *Drylongso.* New York: The New Press, 1993.

Hadjor, Kofi Buenor. *Another America: The Politics of Race and Blame.* Boston; South End Press, 1995.

Hare, Nathan. *The Black Anglo-Saxons.* Chicago: Third World Press, 1991.

hooks, bell. "Dialectically Down with the Critical Program" in Michelle Wallace's *Black Popular Culture.* Gina Dent, ed., Seattle: Bay Press, 1992

_____. *Outlaw Culture.* New York: Routeledge, 1994.

Huggins, Nathan Irvin. *Voices of the Harlem Renaissance.* New York: Oxford University Press, 1976.

Hunter, James David. *Culture Wars: The Struggle to Define America.* New York: Harper Collins Publishers, 1991.

Ingraham, Cynthia L. "Music As The Message: Rap, Hip Hop and R&B Stylings Draw Youth into the Pews." *about ...time Magazine.* (31 December 1998), 22.

Islam, True. *How Came the Black God, Mr. Muhammad?* Vol.1. Atlanta: All in All Publishing, 1997.

Jackson, Robert Scoop. *The Last Black Mecca*. New York: Research Associates School Times Publication, 1998.

Joyce, Donald Franklin. *Gatekeepers of Black Culture: Black-Owned Book Publishing in the United States, 1817-198*. London: Greenwood Press, 1983.

Kelley, Robin D.G. *Yo Mama's Disfunktional!: Fighting the Culture Wars in Urban America*. Massachusetts: Beacon Press, 1997.

Kitwana, Bakari. *The Rap on Gangsta Rap*. Chicago: Third World Press, 1995.

Lee, Martyn J. *Consumer Culture Reborn: The Cultural Politics of Consumption*. New York: Routledge, 1993.

Lipscomb, Michael, and KRS-One. "Can the Teacher be Taught?" *Transitions 57*. (1992), 168-189.

Lomax, Louis E. *When The Word is Given: A report on Elijah Muhammad, Malcolm X, and the Black Muslim World*. New York: The World Publishing Company, 1963.

Marsh, Clifton E. *From Black Muslim to Muslim: The Resurrection, Transformation, and Change of the Lost Found Nation of Islam in America, 1930- 1995*. London: Scarecrow Press, 1996.

Merelman, Richard M. *Representing Black Culture*. New York: Routledge Press, 1995.

Muhammad, Elijah. *Message to the Blackman in America*. Atlanta: Messenger Elijah Muhammad Propagation Society.

Nachias, David. *Research Methods in the Social Sciences*. New York: St. Martin's Press, 1992.

Ohmann, Richard. *Selling Culture: Magazines, Markets, and Class at the Turn of the Century*. New York: Verso Press, 1996.

Parenti, Michael. *Inventing Reality: The Politics of the Mass Media*. New York; St. Martin's Press, 1986.

Perkins, William E. *Droppin' Science: Critical Essays on Rap Music and Hip Hop Culture*. Philadelphia: Temple University, 1996

_____. "Nation of Islam Ideology in the Rap of Public Enemy," *The Emergency of Black and the Emergency of Rap*. Special Issue of *Black Sacred Music: A Journal of Theomusicology*. Jon Michael Spencer, ed., 5:1 North Carolina: Duke University Press, 1991.

Potter, Russell. *Spectacular Vernaculars: Hip-Hop and the Politics of Postmodernism*. Albany State University of New York: 1995, 63.

Prince-A-Cuba. *Our Mecca Is Harlem: Clarence 13X (Allah) and the Five Percent* Hampton: U.B & U.S. Communications Systems, Inc., 1994.

Radin, Margaret Jane. *Contested Commodities.* Massachusetts: Harvard University Press, 1996.

Ro, Ronin. *Gangsta: Merchandising the Rhymes of Violence.* New York: St. Martin's Press, 1996.

Rose, Tricia. *Black Noise.* New Hampshire: University Press of New England, 1994.

_____. *Black Noise: Rap Music and Black Culture in Contemporary America.* London: Wesleyan University Press, 1994.

_____. "Culture Survivalism and the Marketplace Subversions," *In Language, Rhythm, and Sound.* Joseph K. Adjaye and Adriane Andrews eds., Pittsburgh: University of Pittsburgh Press, 1997.

_____. "Hidden Politics: Discursive and Institutional Policing of Rap Music" in *Droppin' Science: Critical Essays on Rap Music and Hip Hop Culture,* William Eric Perkins, ed., Philadelphia: Temple University Press, 1996.

Ross, Andrew. *No Respect: Intellectuals and Popular Culture.* New York: Routledge Press, 1989.

Scott, James C. *Domination and the Arts of Resistance.* New Haven: Yale University Press, 1990.

Smitherman, Geneva. "The Chains Remain the Same: Communicative Practices in the Hip Hop Nation," *Journal of Black Studies.* vol. 28, September 1997.

Spencer, Jon Michael. *The Emergency of Black and the Emergence of Rap.* North Carolina: Duke University Press, 1991.

Stanley, Lawrence. *Rap: The Lyrics.* New York: Penguin Books, 1992.

Tate, Greg. *Flyboy in the Buttermilk.* New York: Simon and Schuster, 1992.

Toop, David. *The Rap Attack: African Jive to New York Hip-Hop.* Boston: South End Press, 1984.

Thomas, Don. "In Hip Hop, Sisters are Doing it for Themselves." *New York Beacon.* vols. 17, 29.

Watkins, S. Craig. *Representing Hip Hop Culture and the Production of Black Cinema.* Chicago: The University of Chicago Press, 1998.

Interviews

Allah, Katema. Interview with author, January 2000. Tape recording.

Allah, Shahid M. Interview with author, May 1998. Tape recording.

B Wise. Interview with author, June 1999, New York. Tape recording.

Born God Allah. Interview with author, July 1999, New York. Tape recording.

D.A.B.L.O. (Christian Hip Hop artist). Interview with author, January 2001. Tape recording.

Divine Ruler Equality Allah. Interview with author, December 2001. Tape recording.

DJ Half Pint. Interview with author, November 2000. Telephone interview.

James, Darryl (owner of Rap Sheet Magazine). Interview with author, January 2001. Tape recording.

Scientific Allah. Interview with author, June 1999, New York. Tape recording.

Understanding God Allah (U-God). Interview with author, December 2001. Tape recording.

INDEX

120 degrees of knowledge 46

AACP (African-American cultural Productions) 1

Adams, Yolanda 67

African 1-6, 8, 9, 11, 12, 15, 20, 22-24, 27-29, 32, 33, 35-37, 40-42, 47, 49, 58, 60-62, 65, 67, 75, 77, 83, 89, 99, 117-119, 123, 126

African-American 2, 3, 6, 22, 35-37, 83, 99, 117, 118, 123

African-American Islam 29

Afrika Bambaataa 21, 40, 41, 56

Afrocentrism 22, 23, 31

Agencies 7, 9, 18, 23, 24, 26, 30, 34, 50-52, 54, 82, 84, 88, 125

Agenda 2000 51

Allah 37, 38, 43, 46, 52, 55, 57, 62

Allah School in Mecca 52

Allen Jr., Ernest 30

Allen, Diane 129

Allen, Harry 30

AM. Diabetes Walk-A-Thon 85

American Red Cross Tupac Blood Drive 85

Americorps Celebration 85

Anderson, Claud 110

Arbitron 82, 83

Artists 1-3, 7, 8, 10, 11, 19, 21, 22, 29-31, 34, 44, 46, 47, 49-53, 56-59, 61-63, 65-67, 69, 70, 73, 78, 79, 81, 83, 84, 91, 93, 95-100, 102, 104, 106-109, 113, 119, 121-123, 127-130

Atlanta 10, 11, 73, 74, 77, 78, 82, 84-86, 88, 93, 97, 98, 100, 102, 104, 113, 114

Atlanta city council 102

Atlanta Hawks Toy Drive 85

Atlanta Hip Hop Coalition 104

Atlanta University Center 10, 11, 113

Attendance Competition 2000 86

AUHC 98, 102, 109-111

Bakari Kitwana 28

Baraka, Amiri 2, 31

B-Boy Summit 100

Beats and Lyrics 78

bell hooks 4
Bernal, Martin 68
BET 49, 69, 70
Bible 30, 31, 59, 63, 65, 68
Billboard 58, 82
Black Commercial Broadcast Ownership 75
Black leadership 57
Black music 6, 28, 32, 67
Black Nationalism 21, 22, 24, 48, 50, 95, 110
Black radio 6, 7, 57, 73-77, 79, 81, 83, 85, 87, 89, 91, 95
Black Star 49, 95, 97
Black Theology 33-35, 37, 39, 41, 43, 45, 47, 49, 51, 53, 55, 57, 59, 61, 63, 66
Black thought 110
Brand Nubian 46
Brooks, Gwendolyn 2
Brown, Morris 113, 114
Cameron, Ryan 86, 87
Cardinale, Gerald 129
Career Fair.Com Live Event 85
Christian Hip Hop 64-67, 69-71, 90
Christian Rap 65
Christianity 6, 36, 41, 65-67, 69, 71, 90
Chuck D 6, 31, 103, 108
Clarence 13x 38-40, 52
Clark Atlanta University 113, 114
Clinton, Bill 130
Colonial Model 16, 105
commodification 4, 7, 12, 13, 16, 27, 107

Common 5, 6, 20, 41, 50, 97, 101
Control Formats 81, 82
cultural imperialism 17
Daryl Aamaa Nubyahn 56
De La Soul 97
Death Row Records 31, 129, 130
Def Jam 127
Dekalb College Voter Registration 85
Didactic nihilism 47-50, 61, 64, 66, 84, 87, 90, 93, 96, 98, 128, 131
DJ Kool Herc 21
DuBois, W. E. B. 132
Dyson, Michael Eric 70
Eagle Scout Health Fair 85
Ear Wax 110
Easton, David 125
Edwin Moses Huggs Run 85
Egleston Scottish Rite Gingerbread Contest 85
Elijah Muhammad 37, 40, 42, 44, 46, 51, 62-64
Equality 45-47, 62
Erykah Badu 58
Ethic 9, 33, 59-64, 71
Evander Holyfield Pep Rally 85
Father Allah 37, 38, 55
FCC regulations 81
Five Percenters (5%) 30, 41, 60
Franklin, Kirk 67
Freaknik 78
G.O.D. 53
GA State Community Service Day 85

Gamma Epsilon Society Cotillion Ball 85

gangsta rap 18, 21, 23, 79, 129, 130

Garvey, Marcus Mosiah 2, 62

Gavin, Bill 82

George, Nelson 21, 28, 60

Giovanni, Nikki 2

Giuliani, Rudolph 99

good health 60, 63

Goodie Mob 62, 97

GOP 129

Gore, Tipper 130

Gospel Music 66, 67, 70, 71, 91

government regulations 73

Graffiti 20, 21, 31, 100, 101, 105

Grandmaster Flash 21, 40

Hall, Pamela D. 17

Hands on Atlanta Day 85

Harlem Renaissance 1, 4, 31

Harris, Donald 105

Henderson, Errol A. 22

Hip Hop Appreciation Week 97

Hip Hop Culture (HC) 4, 11, 12, 18, 25, 33, 35, 37, 39, 41, 43, 45, 47, 49, 51, 53, 55-57, 59, 61, 63, 79, 95, 97, 99, 101, 103-105, 107, 109, 111, 122, 125, 127, 129, 131

historical continuity 6, 18, 20

Holiday Clothing Drive@ Greenbriar Mall 85

Hosea Williams Feed the Hungry Live Broadcast 85

Hot 97.5 "Rocks the Vote" 85

Hot 97.5 Arthritis Foundation's Mini-Grand Prix 85

Hot 97.5 Hair Cuts for the Holidays 85

Hot 97.5 Mayor's Celebrity Softball Game 85

Hot Shots Diabetes B-Ball Game 85

Hot Shots for Hope Game 85

Hughes, Cathy 75

ideal 36, 52

ideology 2, 6, 9, 22, 23, 29, 30, 33, 34, 38, 54-58, 81, 106, 109, 110, 114, 119

Jackson, John G. 68

Jesus 59, 66, 68, 71

Jones, Mack H. 15

Justice 33, 35, 38, 45, 46, 57, 62, 66, 98

keep it real 49, 50

Kemetic origin of Christianity 67

King, Martin Luther 56

Koran 30, 51, 59

KRS-One 63, 67

KUDL 74

Legislation 76, 129, 130

Lomax, Louis E. 36

Lost Found Lesson No.2 45

Love and Understanding Benefit 85

Madhubuti, Haki 2

Malcolm X 36, 37, 39, 42, 44, 56

manifesto 33, 95, 96, 111

Manifesto 33, 95, 96, 111

Mark Anthony Neal 19

Marsh, Clifton E. 36

Mary Mary 67

McCloud, Aminah Beverly 55

McClurkin, Donnie 67
Mills, C. Wright 8
Minority Telecommunications Development Program (MTDP) 75
Mobiltrak 84
Money Talks Seminar 85
Morehouse College 114
Morgan, Joan 69
Mos Def 52, 97
Moses, Robert 25
MTV 49, 56
muslim 36, 42, 46, 51, 55, 127
Napster 107, 108
Nation of Gods and Earths 30, 34, 37
Nation of Islam (NOI) 22, 29, 34, 36, 34-57, 59, 60, 62-64, 95, 106
National Political Caucus of Black Women 129
Neal, Larry 2
Nielsen 82
Nightline 79
nihilism 28, 47-50, 59, 61, 64, 66, 71, 84, 87, 89, 90, 93, 96-98, 111, 128, 131
NOIPAC 51
obscenity laws 129
ODB 100
Official Atlanta Rock the Vote Station 85
Parental Advisory Stickers 130
Perkins, William Eric 21
Pharaoh Monch 97
Pohlman, Marcus 126
political economy 75, 77, 79, 81-83, 85, 87, 89, 91, 104

Political instrument 5, 6, 9-11, 30, 33, 54, 94
Political philosophy 8-11, 30, 32-34, 36, 42, 43, 45-47, 50, 52, 55, 58, 59, 62, 63, 73, 91, 97, 98, 106, 109-111, 113, 123
political system 9, 11, 13, 29, 113, 117, 119, 125-129, 131
Political theory 42
political viability 11, 17, 29, 30, 113
Poor Righteous Teachers 53, 59
Post Industrialism 18, 25, 27, 29, 40, 99
Prison monomorium project 129
Project Phoenix 85
Proposition 187
Proposition 209 101
Proposition 21 101, 127
Proposition 227 101
Public Enemy 21, 22, 29, 31, 56, 57, 97, 103, 108
public policy 9, 125, 126
Public Service Announcement (PSA) 80
Queen Latifah 53
Race music 74
Radio One 75, 85
Radio programming 73, 74, 77, 89
radio station ownership 73
Rage Against the Machine 100
Rap the Vote 99, 126, 127
Rapstation.com 110
REACH 53, 65, 69, 71, 88
Read Across Atlanta 85

Religion 6, 29, 30, 33, 35-37,
   40, 68, 94
Rhythm and Vibes 81
RIAA 107, 108
Rose, Tricia 25, 99
Run DMC 69
Sanchez, Sonia 2
Simmons, Russell 127
Sista Souljah 31
social science 15, 16, 29, 32, 93
Solar Panel 53
SoundScan 66, 83
Spelman College 113, 114
Spiritual Minded 69
statement of ideals 9, 46
Supreme mathematics 46
Talib Kweli 95
Tate, Greg 31
Tax Day Preparation @ Green-
   briar Mall 85
The Bomb 81
The Gavin Report 82
*The Mis-Education of the
   Negro* 62
The Nation Time Syndicate
   (NTS) 103, 104
*The Parents Music Resource
   Center* 130
*The Telecommunication Act of
   1996* 76
The Word 36, 39, 47, 52, 57,
   71
Third Eye Movement 101
Thompson, Robert Farris 20
Timba 94
Toop, David 31
Traditional model 107, 108
Tucker, C. Delores 129

Tu-Pac Shakur 100
Underground Hip Hop (UHC)
   93-98, 101, 102, 104-106,
   107, 109-111
Universal Negro Improvement
   Association (UNIA) 2
urban renewal projects 41
V-103 88
viable political instrument 5, 6,
   9, 11, 30, 54
Vintage Imperial 98
Vinyl Junkies 98
Watkins, S. Craig 19
WB 36 "DO Something" Event
   85
WDIA 74
WERD 74
West, Cornel 127
WGES 74
white negro 79
Wilson, William Julius 105
Winans 67, 70
WRAS 77, 80, 81, 90
WRFG 77, 80, 90, 104, 110
Wu Tang Clan
WVEE 77, 85, 90
WWRL 74
X-Clan 21
Zulu Kings 42
Zulu Nation 42